Word Savvy

Integrated Vocabulary, Spelling, & Word Study, Grades 3–6

Max Brand

Stenhouse Publishers
Portland, Maine

Stenhouse Publishers
www.stenhouse.com

Credits

Page 33: "Saving National Parks" from *Exploring Nonfiction* series. Copyright © *Time for Kids,* a Time Inc. Company. Used with permission.

Page 65: "Walking," from *Ordinary Things* by Ralph Fletcher. Copyright © 1997 by Ralph Fletcher. Reprinted with the permission of Atheneum Books for Young Readers, an imprint of Simon & Schuster Children's Publishing Division. All rights reserved.

Page 66: "The Bully" from *Baseball, Snakes, and Summer Squash* by Donald Graves. Copyright © 1996 by Donald Graves. Reprinted with permission of Boyds Mills Press. All rights reserved.

Page 132: "Whiteout" from *Exploring Nonfiction* series. Copyright © *Time for Kids,* a Time Inc. Company. Used with permission.

Page 162: "maple syrup buckets," from *Ordinary Things* by Ralph Fletcher. Copyright © 1997 by Ralph Fletcher. Reprinted with the permission of Atheneum Books for Young Readers, an imprint of Simon & Schuster Children's Publishing Division. All rights reserved.

Library of Congress Cataloging-in-Publication Data
Brand, Max, 1958–
    Word savvy : integrated vocabulary, spelling, and word study, grades 3–6 / Max Brand.
        p. cm.
        Includes bibliographical references.
        ISBN 1-57110-366-X (alk. paper)
        1. Language arts (Elementary) 2. Vocabulary—Study and teaching (Elementary) 3. English language—Orthography and spelling—Study and teaching (Elementary) I. Title.
LB1576.B583 2004
372.61—dc22   2003070380

Manufactured in the United States of America on acid-free paper
10 09 08 07 06 05 04 9 8 7 6 5 4 3 2 1

*In memory of my mother, Lillian,
and my grandmother Bella and their simple words,
"We should all live and be well."*

Contents

Foreword

In *Word Savvy: Integrated Vocabulary, Spelling, and Word Study, Grades 3–6,* Max Brand paints a vivid picture of life in his classroom. As I read, I found that his students spoke with authority as writers and "word-smiths." Max tells the revealing story of his journey to understand the mystery of how children learn language, vocabulary, and spelling. His classroom is a special world where children develop "word-savvy" strategies that they use as they read, write, and study within a dynamic curriculum. Within these pages, classroom teachers will find the support they need to expand their own repertoires for teaching about vocabulary, word study, and spelling. Max has dedicated his professional teaching career to helping children become strategic with words, their use, and their spelling. He creates experiences that help students marvel about and question words and their derivations to explore precise meanings.

The stance that Max has taken in this book is of critical importance for classroom teachers in grades three through six. In today's world of high-stakes assessment, it is all too easy to relegate word learning to rote memorization and skills exercises (maybe on the computer!). The long-term results of these practices, however, do not lead to strategic spellers who can independently learn about the vast vocabulary in the English language. Erhi (1992) described the limitations of rote learning:

> What students store in memory about specific words' spellings is regulated in part by what they know about the general system. Learners who lack this knowledge are left with rote memorization, which takes longer and is more easily forgotten. Similarly, what students learn about the orthographic system evolves in part from the accumulation of experiences with specific word spellings. (p. 308)

The methods described in *Word Savvy* are based on the belief that learners grow in their understanding of vocabulary and spelling over time as they encounter and study words in a variety of settings. Donald

Bear and his colleagues write about the importance of this belief in their classic text *Words Their Way:*

> Getting good at word recognition, spelling, and vocabulary is not just a matter of memorizing isolated rules and definitions. The best way to develop fast, accurate perception of word features is to engage in meaningful reading and writing, and to have multiple opportunities to examine those same words out of context, in isolation, in all their glory. The most effective instruction in phonics, spelling, and vocabulary links word study to the texts being read, provides a systematic scope and sequence of word-level skills, and provides multiple opportunities for hands-on practice. (Bear et al. 2003, p. 4)

These are the techniques that are brought to life in Max Brand's classroom and fully described in *Word Savvy.* As one of his students writes, "Word study helps us in everyday life. We are expanding our vocabularies, learning about syllable breaks, when to drop and add letters, and word comprehension." In his apprenticeship model, Max uses poetry, content area texts, children's literature, and particular student engagements throughout the day to immerse students in word learning. He sees his role as making the implicit ways words work more explicit within the classroom culture.

Another important contribution of this text is the ongoing links that Max makes with the theory, the research on spelling and vocabulary, and his own classroom practices. In this way, he encourages teachers to think with him, learn with him, and explore the wonder of his students' learning. Max describes his beginning steps in using observation and engagements such as Read like a Writer, Stretch the Sketch, and Have a Go to kick off word study in the first weeks of school. The careful way he presents lessons and relates them to theory and research will aid classroom teachers in stretching with him to make word study a successful enterprise with their own students. Max leads his students to rethink and value spelling, to develop vocabulary, and to link learning across the curriculum.

Max makes a unique contribution in this book in that he shows how students are integral to his own learning. He quotes the students, provides samples of their work, and shows each of us as teachers what it means to "follow your students" in making instructional decisions.

I am proud to write this foreword. I've had the pleasure of working alongside Max since he was an undergraduate student. I've seen him grow, marry, have children, and become a highly reflective instructional leader. He is a lifelong learner passing on a proud legacy to his students—and yours.

Diane E. DeFord

Acknowledgments

Spirit is a magical word that has myriad meanings I've discovered while investigating and writing about becoming word-savvy. Gayle, my wife, has been the guiding spirit that has kept this book fresh for me each night while I've pecked at the keyboard. She has maintained a household of three boys, extra chores, and countless readings of drafts. Her insight and thoughtful questions helped re-vision my thinking as she anticipated questions I would never have dreamed of. No one could be a better first editor, mother, soul mate, and wife.

The teachers and students whose voices danced in my mind have really helped shape my thinking. I appreciate all the teachers who opened their doors to me while I was a district coordinator and allowed me to work with their students. The questions your students asked and our dialogue were critical in helping me write a user-friendly text. Of course, my fifth-grade classes have really been helpful as we have explored the boundaries of what it means to play with words each day. My students have adopted and challenged me with my own "Why?"

Mentors along the way have been important in reshaping my thinking. Jan Bates has been more than a mentor; she has been a surrogate mother, coach, and friend. The wonderful staff at Ohio State University has always helped me envision possibilities in education. I have been fortunate to have been influenced by Diane DeFord, Gay Su Pinnell, Carol Lyons, Rob Tierney, and others.

The groundwork that Don Graves laid with his seminal book *Writing: Teachers and Children at Work* has had a profound effect on my thinking. Ralph Fletcher has not only been a mentor to me but has mentored my students with his poetry, picture books, and children's novels. Thanks for your writing tip while in transit to the airport—words of wisdom that propelled my writing during those dry times.

Franki Sibberson and that chance phone call led to a friendship and our becoming colleagues. She now has to listen to my daily banter as I explore my thinking about teaching and learning. Tom Bates, my principal, has been a role model as he demonstrates daily what it means to lead by example. The fifth-grade staff at Eli Pinney understands me and allows me to be myself. Thanks, Aida, Bonnie, and Tom.

The thoughtful and enthusiastic ideas that Jennifer Allen provided were timely and kept me focused while drafting. Amy Smedley and Cathy Mere are part of animated and never-seeming-to-end conversations about what is best for kids. Martha Drury's insightful design allows my students' voices to be heard.

Brenda Power, there are not enough meanings for *thank you*. Moving from a phone conversation to this book never seemed possible, yet you always kept the rudder steering me toward the final destination, this book.

My father and sisters were very supportive as we rummaged through fifty years of household possessions and rekindled Brand family memories. My father got me to read *Sports Illustrated* and discover authors playing with fantastic words. My sister Ellen read drafts and posed questions only a big sister would dare to ask.

Max, Joel, and Jon were curious about what their father was doing sequestered in his office during summer vacation. Their dinnertime banter is always filled with word wonders. Thanks for giving me time to think, write, and learn.

Introduction: Word-Savvy Thinking

I think spelling tests are unnessecary. *Do you know why? In the third grade I had a spelling test and one of the words was* nessecary. *I memorized it for the week and got it right for the test, but now in fifth grade I know I spell it wrong all the time. That's a perfect example. They don't help me remember the words for life.*

Kelsey

I recently helped my father clean out his house as he prepared to move. While throwing boxes from the basement into a dumpster, I came across my fourth-grade progress report. I studied my grades, noting a dramatic improvement in spelling. Amazingly, I went from being a C speller during the first grading period to an A speller the remaining three grading periods.

Upon further examination, I noticed that my work habits were judged "weak," hinting that with a bit of effort I could improve my grades. I recall my concerned parents making me sit at the kitchen table night after night studying weekly spelling lists. Studying weekly lists helped me boost my grade, but did it help my writing? My English grade did not get better over the course of the year: "improvement needed."

My proud parents had also held on to my composition book that was periodically used for writing stories. The last piece of voiceless writing had the following spelling errors: *fined* for *find, bot* for *bought, tride* for *tried, there* for *their, screming* for *screaming, bleading* for *bleeding, finilly* for *finally,* and *fiteing* for *fighting.* I think these errors demonstrate that I was not an A speller.

Over the years, I have watched my own students dutifully study spelling lists, spell words correctly on tests, look up the meaning of unfamiliar words in the dictionary, but still not understand how to use this knowledge as they wrote or thought about the books they read. Thinking about my old progress report, I found it interesting how spelling was graded as a separate subject.

I have learned that teaching kids *about* words cannot be separated from *using* words. Each content area has a rich and varied vocabulary that students learn to use as they demonstrate their growing understanding of concepts in these areas. Language learning is the foundation of the school curriculum. Teaching kids how to look at and think about words in meaningful contexts extends across the curriculum. I know that while I am writing in front of my students, demonstrating how to craft an introductory paragraph, there is a meaningful opportunity to make explicit when to use *their* or *there* as well as to clarify when to use *than* instead of *then.*

Brock highlights words and concepts from a nonfiction text in his writing notebook.

My thinking about words has gradually changed as I have moved from being a classroom teacher, literacy coordinator, district language arts coordinator, and now back to the classroom as a fifth-grade teacher. As my thinking has changed, my goal for word learning has changed. I want my students not only to learn how to spell words and learn vocabulary skills but to develop strategies for using these skills as they read, write, and learn a complex content curriculum.

What Is Word Study?

I think word study is where you learn how to spell words and how to tell words apart like there, their, *and* they're *or* effect *and* affect. *It also helps you know where to put them in a sentence and know what they mean.*

Matt

Word study has become an umbrella term used to describe teaching practices related to word knowledge. Teaching this knowledge supports students as they develop fluency and understanding in their reading, as well as the ability to craft thoughtful writing. An effective word study system helps students develop an understanding of orthography, vocabulary, word recognition, and decoding strategies.

I am still trying to solve the mystery of how kids learn about language, vocabulary, and spelling. Some students seem to exert almost no effort, whereas others are challenged and frustrated by all their labors. My goal is for students to become word-savvy—to develop an understanding of how words work within the context of reading and writing, and to become excited about words as they learn to manipulate them in playful ways.

I ask myself, What does the word-savvy student do each day? Donald Murray (1996) best describes what a word-savvy student might look and sound like during the school day. He writes, "I spend my mornings messing around in language, learning the rules and then breaking them, making up words, listening to the beat and melody of language, putting in and taking out, fitting and shaping, moving and removing, playing language into meaning" (6). The word-savvy student is curious about words as she marvels about and questions words she hears, reads, and writes.

I also try to follow Ralph Fletcher's (1993) advice: "As teachers, we can share with students the pleasure in finding the precise words to communicate the nuance of thought. We can encourage students to play naturally with language. And we can celebrate their language breakthroughs whenever they occur" (38). When I think of curriculum, I think of word-learning opportunities.

A Balanced Approach: Word Learning Across the Day

Word study helps us in everyday life. We are expanding our vocabularies, learning about syllable breaks, when to drop and add letters, and word comprehension. It's not fun, but we need it. As I write this, I am using my word study knowledge.

Dan

I often reflect on the mandates and perceptions of instruction posed by state standards, district curricula, and the community regarding word knowledge. Do people really believe that we are not addressing orthographic, phonetic, and vocabulary knowledge? While we teach children to write and read, students' attention has to be directed toward print.

It is the emphasis we already place on print that may be a bit out of balance. The push in literacy instruction feels like it is moving us as teachers to more attention to print, with less emphasis on understanding. This is in opposition to what we know about our students and the

Brienna reads under a wall of interesting words and lines found by students during independent reading time.

difficulties they experience during testing. They can read the words, but they do not understand what they read. We have students who can write to a prompt but do not understand how to use written language as a tool of thought. The only way I know to deal with this issue is to balance the curriculum to include word study throughout the day. This probably sounds a bit lofty and complicated, but my approach is really very practical.

While planning for word study, I think about state standards, district curricula, essential word study concepts, and notes made while browsing students' work. I consider where in the day there are opportunities for explicit instruction and support that will help my students learn about words. I do have a designated word study block (fifteen minutes) where mini-lessons, activities, and feedback are provided.

But this time alone is not enough to help students become word-savvy. My students need to be supported as they develop a taste for words as well as the desire to discover and uncover the mystery of words. They need multiple experiences thinking about spelling and vocabulary throughout the day as they encounter print. I find my day is full of word-learning opportunities. The challenge is deciding which ones will enable students to grow in their understanding of words.

Teaching and Learning Words: The Basics

Weird words catch my eye because the words are usually made up, long, funny, foreign, or even I can't understand them. If I'm reading and I come across one, I usually stop and repeat the word in my head and think about how it was used. Then I would write it down in my WORDS category on my thinking sheet. I wonder and think if my word is interesting enough to go on the wall.

Laura

Studying birds and words are renewed passions in my life. My wife, Gayle, our three sons, and I recently moved into the dream house of our courting years. The house is nestled in a wooded area lined with meandering trails and filled with many birds.

I often use the book *Birds of Ohio* by Stan Tekiela as a guide, and his words of wisdom: "Identifying birds isn't as difficult as you might think. If you follow just a few basic strategies, you can increase your chances of successfully identifying most birds you see! One of the first and easiest things to do when you see a new bird is to note its color." While I wander through the woods, I've learned to quickly note the birds that regularly fly in and out of sight. Many of these same birds frequent the feeder outside my kitchen window, so even my son Jon at 3½ recognizes them and can name them.

The birds I see less frequently during my daily walks are more difficult to name at a glance. The more time I spend on the trail using my thumb-worn guidebook to help train my eye where to look and what to look for, the more proficient I become at identifying less frequent visitors that fly through our yard and woods.

While on the trail I carry my bird field guide, writer's notebook, and pen. I sketch, label, and write notes about my observations as I continue to grow in my understanding of birds. As I have been thinking and learning about birds, the process has become synonymous with my thinking about teaching, learning, and understanding words.

A Theory of Learning Words

What makes me notice words is if they are big or different languages, or if I can't pronounce them. What I usually do if it's big is think about what the word is and the purpose it is serving.

Jackie

Word knowledge involves decoding, vocabulary, and spelling. Learning about words and their use requires the learner to read, write, and think with an eye on them. I think of the teacher's role as similar to a seasoned trail guide—a guide who has traversed the same trails over and over, thinking more deeply about what she notices each time. Enthusiasm is created for those around the guide as she shares her expertise, passion, and learning with hikers. "The role assumed by the teacher is that of knowledgeable guide, rather than that of prime dispenser of information and arbiter of what is correct" (Stevenson and Stigler 1992, 177).

I assume the role of a well-informed guide of word/language knowledge for my fifth-grade students. I am deliberate as I think through what word knowledge is and where, when, and how this knowledge is to be used and taught. I guide students as they develop an eye for noticing word features, increasing their vocabularies while applying word knowledge purposefully for the myriad of reasons students read, write, and spell each day.

Oral language is the web that binds complex learning to the diverse needs of students. "For literacy, meaningful discourse is both destination and vehicle" (Tharp and Gallimore 1988, 93). The physical and social dynamics of my classroom need to allow for plenty of talk.

In designing my classroom, I have adopted an apprenticeship model to guide my students toward specific learning outcomes. I have tried to adapt Cambourne's (2002) philosophy of learning in this approach. The three underlying premises of this approach are

- To immerse learners in a cultural activity
- To make explicit what is implicit
- To organize learning around a body of knowledge

I try from the first day of school to set up a safe, risk-free environment in which both explicit and informal instruction occurs. Students learn how to listen, talk, and develop vocabulary that is used in creating shared and unique understanding. Listening, speaking, reading, writing, and spelling are developed over time.

The cultural activity of literacy includes the concept of word knowledge, especially as it relates to helping students with their reading and writing. I am responsible for organizing, designing, and clearly explaining the purpose of instruction and the learning environment. My students and I are responsible for maintaining this learning community. Fountas and Pinnell (2001) note how crucial these learning communities are: "Students learn best if they are part of a community in which all members take responsibility for their own learning and also for one another's learning. Creating that learning community takes time and organization, but the payoff is great" (88).

My investigation into my own word learning while I read, write, and converse with my family, colleagues, friends, and students has helped me clarify my thinking. The challenge of creating a classroom culture is that I am trying to replicate natural learning in an unnatural environment. So, when I think about designing a word-savvy classroom culture, I begin by examining my own word-learning practices. The following practices have shaped my thinking:

- I collect words from multiple media and record them in my writing notebook.
- I check the spelling of words that usually are misspelled.
- I use multiple strategies to help me fix my spelling (e.g., write on sticky notes to determine spelling that looks correct, consult spell-check or dictionary).
- I use word parts to help infer word meanings.
- I use background knowledge and context to help me infer word meanings.
- I create word webs of related words in my writing notebook.
- I reread my writing carefully, considering my word selection in relation to the message I'm trying to convey.

If I want to apprentice my students into what Frank Smith (1988) calls "the literacy club," I need to demonstrate how to live that life. The learning tool that I use for my personal word study is my notebook. It has helped me expand my vocabulary and develop my writing skills, and it serves as a resource. Daily I explore and think as I write in my notebook. I also use my notebook to plan for instruction and record observations of my classroom.

Over the years my notebook has become an extension of my left hand. I feel comfortable taking notes as my students and I discuss, reflect, plot, evaluate, and plan where to go next. I have found that as I am recording my thoughts, seed ideas begin to emerge as I think about what is next. Conferring with students and parents or preparing grade cards is not as time-consuming since I have kept a running account of each child in my notebook. It is less stressful now to plan for parent conferences and tell parents what they can do to help their child. I know where the children have been with their learning and where we are headed. My planning notebook is the tool that helps me match student needs with curriculum objectives.

Students also use notebooks as tools to help them think and learn about words, and to partake in a variety of word-learning activities. Students use their notebooks when introduced to graphic organizers while learning to infer word meanings, when collecting words to support their writing, and during spelling activities. They keep frequently mis-

I confer with a small group of students, noting their thinking in my planning notebook.

spelled words in a word bank they have attached in the back cover of their word study notebooks.

Word Knowledge Model

When I am looking for words I try to find words that are unique, funny, and interesting. I stop and try to think about its meaning, its uniqueness, its place in a book, and more. That's how I choose my words.

Sydney

To aid in crafting my word study lessons, I have tried to organize my knowledge of words into three groups: sound, pattern, and meaning (see Figure 1.1). Students' orchestration of sound, pattern, and meaning is fundamental to their understanding of words.

Sound

Sounds surround us. The ear has become attuned to sounds in the environment and sorted them since birth. The mother's voice, the father's voice, other voices heard over and over again become familiar and

Figure 1.1 Word knowledge.

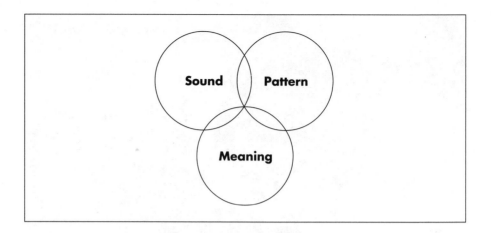

recognizable. A baby's brain sorts, sifts through, and categorizes a range of other sounds unique to each family as well as household noises like a vacuum cleaner's buzz.

Preschool and kindergarten children often play with sounds, even as they begin to direct their attention to learning letters and letter sounds while developing phonemic awareness. Young children's earliest attempts at writing may grow from this letter knowledge as they use a single letter or letter names to represent a word (*K, KT, KAT, CAT*). Young children also learn to systematically segment and record the names of letters to represent sounds in their temporary spelling attempts.

Each year a handful of students enters intermediate grades relying on letter sounds as their primary spelling and reading strategy when encountering unknown words. "Sound it out" is the common refrain from many of my students when asked how they spell or read unknown words. Some students' overreliance on this strategy probably has made it difficult for them to develop fluency in their reading and writing.

I wonder if these students really understand how to listen to themselves as they read. Do they realize that their reading should be fluent and make sense? Do these students know how to segment words into parts? Once they have segmented the word, can they attach sound to this part? Can this same student combine the sounds into words while writing? These are questions I use to guide my thinking while observing and conferring with students.

When I think about what is basic to a speller who is developing knowledge of sounds to spell words, the following features are my focus for instruction:

Sound
- Letters and letter sounds
- Consonants

- Short vowels
- Long vowels
- Blends and clusters
- Single-syllable words

I try to help the child not only hear these sounds but also begin to see the patterns of letters that are related to these sounds.

Pattern

Patterns also surround us. The brain searches, compares, contrasts, notes, and remembers patterns. Sight words, word families, syllable breaks, root words, and affixes are important patterns students assimilate as they develop word knowledge. It would be inefficient for students to learn to read and spell letter by letter. Students develop visual memories for common spelling patterns (single-syllable rimes or word families) often encountered in primary-grade reading materials and spelling programs. Students begin to recognize and understand letter groups and their influence on decoding and spelling.

Students can also learn to look for patterns as they read by searching words for known parts. The rimes, syllable groups, prefixes, root words, and endings learned during reading, writing, and word study instruction are useful. Students read and write polysyllabic unknown words implicitly by noticing, articulating, and blending these patterns fluently into sounds, syllables, words, and language. Students develop knowledge of spelling patterns and their influence on meaning as well as their oddities related to origin.

Language learners are searching for order in these patterns as their vocabulary grows more sophisticated. The brain searches for generalities by using exemplars that are familiar and have meaning. These exemplars serve as a model as students examine an unfamiliar written word while reading or writing.

Students at this stage of development need guidance in how to use their understanding of sounds and patterns that represent these sounds. When students attempt to spell unknown words, they need to "have a go," using knowledge of spelling patterns as they learn to monitor whether their spelling attempts look right. Conferring with students helps the children develop an eye for looking at their spelling attempts and confidence in their growing knowledge of how to use spelling patterns.

When I think about what is basic to a speller who is developing knowledge of patterns to spell words, these features are my focus for instruction:

Pattern
- Rimes
- *R*-controlled vowels
- Syllables
- High-frequency words
- Polysyllabic words
- Stressed syllables
- Unstressed syllables
- Drop the *e* and add *-ing* or *-ed*
- Drop the *y* and add *-ies* or *-ied*

I try to help the child not only sort these patterns out but also to learn to look across words, asking, Does this look right?

Meaning

We all try to make sense of the world around us. We use both the sounds and images we have encountered as we try to understand the meaning of what we see, hear, feel, and experience. Children who learn to look for meaning as it relates to words are well on their way to developing independent thinking skills and strategies.

How many times a day does a toddler inquire, What does this mean? Encouraging students to not only ask how to pronounce words but also to monitor for meaning is important. I want my intermediate-grade students to continue to develop and spontaneously play with language, as preschoolers do. Encouraging students to think about why a speaker or author has chosen the words he has to express his thoughts is a good starting place to rebuild excitement about word learning.

When I think about meaning related to word study, it is more than morphology. Vocabulary development is critical to students as they read increasingly challenging texts that are more difficult because of the sophistication of the language (idioms, turns of phrase, and complex vocabulary).

We need to support students as they try to understand the complexities of the written word. I note homophones, root words, affixes, and derivations during reading and writing instruction. Teaching students to look for root words and think about their associated meanings is an important part of my instruction. I teach students how to use root words in a word like *redemptioner* to decode and understand, which is critical for developing meaning-based strategies. Inferring meaning from oral and written language encounters with unknown words helps students develop strategies for figuring out word meanings as they develop their own oral and written vocabulary. Noting the context in which unknown words are found, and how to use this context, is part of the strategy we use on the way to becoming savvy about word meanings.

Students at this stage of development need guidance in how to use their understanding of meaning and root words and affixes as they infer the meaning of challenging vocabulary. I often confer with students, helping them locate and think about the root word in the context of what they are reading.

When I think about what is basic to a speller who is developing knowledge of meaning to spell words and infer the meaning of unknown words, these features are my focus for instruction:

Meaning
- Root words (or base words)
- Affixes
- Word origins
- Word use

I try to help the student think about the root word, what has been added to the root word, and how to use the context that surrounds the word. I also explore the country of origin for words, especially Latin- and Greek-derived words.

Planning for Independence

I think that I do word study all the time. When I ask questions about
pronunciation and what words mean, that's what I consider word study.

Drake

While thinking about supporting my students as they attempt new word study tasks—developing spelling or vocabulary skills and strategies—and coaching them to become independent with this knowledge, I developed a model to guide my teaching. In designing this model I have adapted the thinking behind Brian Cambourne's (1984; 2002) conditions of learning model and Pearson and Gallagher's (1983) gradual release of responsibility model. This model allows me to apprentice my students as they become word-savvy (see Figure 1.2).

When I apprentice a group of learners, the first step in their learning is to *demonstrate*. Demonstration is showing students how. I try to make my demonstrations quick and purposeful because the learners are watching, not actively participating. Demonstrating is designed to create a model that sticks in the back of the students' minds as they begin to understand "how to."

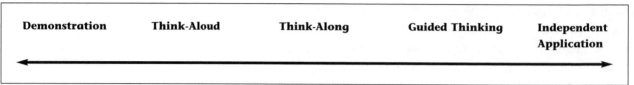

Demonstration	Think-Aloud	Think-Along	Guided Thinking	Independent Application

Figure 1.2 Word apprenticeship learning model. Use of these teaching strategies should be flexible as you lead students toward independence.

The following word study demonstrations have helped students understand how to do a task:

- How to do any new word-learning activity
- How to look across a line of print for spelling errors
- How to self-correct spelling errors
- How to infer the meaning of an unknown word
- How to locate and record important words in a notebook while reading
- How to revise words and lines in writing

Demonstrating is only the first step in supporting my students as they begin to develop skills and strategies. The next step is to build in the rationale for why I am completing a task. I stop at key points of the demonstration and *think aloud,* telling the students what is going through my mind. For example, when I stop to check the spelling of a word like *intermediate,* I might tell the students that as I look across the word, I stop at the second syllable. I may have forgotten to write the *e,* because I write quickly. Students nod their heads as they relate to having done the same thing in their own writing.

When students begin to interrupt my thinking and finish sentences for me during a demonstration, I know they are ready to *think along* with

Demonstration and think-aloud with word web.

Aaron explains to Tim how he used key words from the class chart while writing his book review.

me. During this step I invite the students to participate by sharing their thinking. My students and I work together to complete activities that they could not complete on their own. While using shared reading of a textbook to help students understand how to infer meaning of vocabulary, it is useful to think along with students. Students master the language and rationale for developing these skills and strategies. I have found that during individual conferences, students use the language developed in the think-along activities.

Guided thinking occurs most often during small-group or individual conferences. I guide and prompt students as they try to apply strategies and skills on their own. I know that with some prompting they will be able to complete the task on their own. Conferring with students who are editing spelling errors, I ask them to "look across the word for a part that does not look right." I may have to be even more specific by saying, "Look at each syllable of the word and check to make sure the vowel pattern looks right."

This guiding of students' thinking pushes them toward the ultimate goal, which is *independent application*. I want my students to independently apply what I have taught them through the use of demonstration, thinking aloud, thinking along, or guided thinking. While students are applying this knowledge, my role is to observe, confer, and coach as they learn how to apply the thinking skill to their strategic thinking.

Supporting Intermediate-Grade Students

I absolutely hate spelling tests. They pour stress all over me. Even though I need spelling tests because I can't spell correctly, I still dislike them. They scare me. They embarrass me. When people peek at my corrected sheet they see how many I missed.

Abby

Even though intermediate-grade students come to us with a breadth and depth of word knowledge, they still need supportive instruction. It's tempting to push these students toward independence prior to readiness. We feel pressure to move quickly toward grade-level benchmarks before students have developed self-regulating behaviors. Intermediate-grade students can fool us, demonstrating many competencies. But this doesn't mean they are able to use these skills and strategies in context. By carefully moving them from apprenticeship to independent practice, I scaffold their learning and see where the gaps are in their competencies.

Crafting thoughtful lessons that take into account student understanding allows me to design instruction within students' "zone of proximal development" (Vygotsky 1934). Responsive teaching needs to be planned instead of assigning lists of words that are either memorized or defined. The trick is providing enough help so that the students still remain in control of the strategy and the learning.

Planning for the First Weeks of School

Notebook

Clean white pages,
hungry for words,
thirsty for thoughts,

My mind scattered
over the pages.

A

Fresh

New

Start

The design of sneakers varied little until the 1960s when competitive runners began to turn to lighter-weight shoes. Reducing the weight of shoes clearly improved performance, but problems of traction remained. A running coach, Bill Bowerman, went into the sneaker business in 1962. He paid close attention to the interest in lighter-weight shoes and the problems of traction.

One morning while he was making waffles, he had an idea. He heated a piece of rubber in the waffle iron to produce the first waffle-shaped sole pattern that became the world standard for running shoes. Subsequently, engineers and computers would be used to design and test the best waffle patterns for different athletic purposes. But the initial discovery came from Bowerman's paying attention, being open, making connections, drawing on personal experiences, getting a feel for what was possible, exploration, documenting his initial results, and applying what he learned.

Michael Patton (2002, 203)

The August heat is stifling as the air-conditioning hums non-stop. I promise myself to get organized as the school year inches closer—no longer will notes about lessons and students pile up on my dresser, by week's end becoming indecipherable and as difficult to comprehend as a broken jigsaw puzzle.

As I move into the first weeks of school, I want to get off to a good start. Many students dread spelling and vocabulary learning, especially those who have had difficulty with them over the years. I want students to feel supported as they apply new skills and strategies to their reading and writing. Students need to trust me so that they can take risks, especially with their writing.

I want my students to understand what is expected from them as well as what choices they have as they develop the rituals, routines, and tools of a word-savvy learner. The first six weeks help build the foundation that will allow my students to refine and revise their thinking about words.

My preparation in August begins with general questions:

- What do students need in the first six weeks to become word-savvy?
- What do I want to demonstrate, guide, and coach my students to do independently?

- When will opportunities come up during the day to teach these strategies and skills?
- Which learning context provides me with the chance to be clear and focused with my teaching, and then provide time for students to authentically use and practice their skills?

The challenge is supporting student understanding by using short, focused lessons and then connecting these lessons throughout the day and year. Thinking about all the opportunities that come up in a day, I ask, Where should I plug in these explicit lessons? How do I keep a record of all these plans and student talk?

Organized thinking will help focus my teaching on what is important. Explicit teaching reflecting the needs of the learners has to be more effective than the wadded notes and ancient lesson plans I've used in years past. This all sounds good in the summer, but where to begin?

I start by roughing out a year at a glance based on past experience. "Big ideas" related to language learning, spelling, vocabulary, and decoding skills focus my attention on instructional objectives, types of support necessary, and the learning contexts that reinforce these reading and writing strategies/skills. I also review Ohio's Academic State Standards for Language Arts to ensure that I incorporate these guidelines as well.

My goal is to merge student needs with experiential logic and state standards. In August, I develop a tentative six-week plan. Once students arrive, I will use both informal and formal assessment instruments to learn more about their literacy/language knowledge and adjust my plan. Looking back at old plans, state mandates, and student records, I typically spend the first six to eight weeks reacquainting my class with word-learning concepts (see Figure 2.1).

Using Notes to Plan

Note taking has become a tool that enables me to reflect on and synthesize the complexity of each day's events. My note gathering has become an invaluable model to my students, demonstrating the benefits of notes as a planning and thinking tool. This may sound like a lot of work, but it proves to take less time than many of my colleagues spend correcting stacks of assignments nightly.

While birding I saunter through the woods with a notebook, binoculars, and field guide. I've trained my ears and eyes to help me spy an array of birds during each walk. My birding notebook is a resource that has trained me to quickly note and record observations. By including

---

Spelling
- High-frequency words. Do students misspell high-frequency words? Do students spell these words quickly and automatically?
- Plural confusions. Do students use *s, 's,* and *ies* interchangeably?
- Consonant doubling. Do students double consonants when adding suffixes? Do students spell multisyllable words that have doubled consonants correctly?
- Long vowels. Do students spell most long vowels with a silent *e*? Do students confuse long-vowel patterns?
- Affixes. Do students spell these using visual patterns instead of by sound (e.g., *jumpt/jumped*)?

Vocabulary
- Self-monitoring understanding. Do students realize when they do not know the meaning of a word?
- Appealing for help. Do students ask for help or use a resource when they are unsure of the meaning of a word?
- Context-based strategies. Do students know how to use the context of reading materials or conversation to infer the meaning of an unknown word?
- Word-part strategy. Do students use base or root words or affixes to figure out the meaning of an unknown word (e.g., *redeem/redemptioner*)?
- Synonyms. Do students relate an unknown word to a synonym (e.g., *uppity/stuck up*)?
- Incorporating vocabulary. Do students use new vocabulary during conversations or while writing?

Decoding
- Self-monitoring. Do students listen to themselves while reading orally during a reading conference or reading assessment for miscues?
- Self-repairing. Do students attempt and often correct miscues while reading orally?
- Fluency. Do students anticipate a word based on the meaning of text being read?
- Word part strategies. Do students use knowledge of prefixes, syllable breaks, or root words while orally reading an unknown word?

Figure 2.1 Word-learning concepts to focus on.

markings, color, size, beak or wing shapes along with the location of my sightings, my knowledge about birds and their behaviors has grown. Quick sketches and notes are all I can get during my sightings before I have to move on.

When I return home I study my scribbles and sketches as I attempt to better understand birds that live and visit near my home. I transfer new data into a log that I use to track seasonal and yearly sightings.

Rereading, referring to, and leafing through my birding books helps me become more adept at identifying these shy creatures and their living patterns. Knowing which birds I have seen, where I have seen them, and the seasonal changes in the woods helps me think about future encounters as I prepare for my next daily walk.

This is how I now approach planning, observing, and reflecting in the classroom, especially for word learning. Most of my notebook work occurs during the school day. Nightly, I read and reflect on the notes from my notebook that reflect the day's activities and learning. I use this time to shape the next day's lessons as I try to meet group and individual needs.

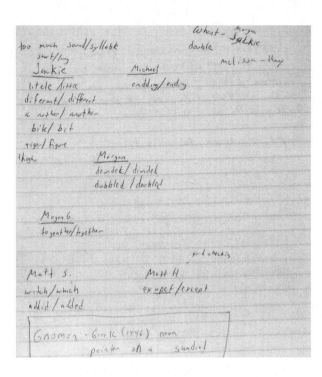

Figure 2.2 A page from my notebook recording students' misspellings and a new word, *gnomon.*

Figure 2.2 shows a page from my planning notebook early in the school year. I record a handful of student misspellings and record a new vocabulary word the group began using—*gnomon,* a name for a sundial that the class discovered during our investigation of the solar system.

I have the following uses for my planning notebook.

Planning Notebook Uses
- Record student conference notes
- Record anecdotal notes about students
- Record student misspellings (about five students per day)
- Record student conversations in large- and small-group settings (paraphrasing the "big ideas")
- Think through and write what big ideas will be focused on during the year
- Think through and write focus for six weeks
- Think through and write weekly goals
- Record lesson plans and then take notes next to them for future consideration
- Model note taking to students

Now I feel naked if I do not have my notebook in tow as I move around the classroom. To simplify and organize my record keeping I use a 5" x 7" notebook, typically one for each grading period. I record a variety of observations, conversations, and anecdotes daily. Snippets of student conversations, oral reading, conference notes, and spelling misunderstandings fill my planning notebook as I prepare for the next day's lessons.

Graham (1999) describes Jean Craighead George's use of notebook entries: "She says that her journal is a 'jerky combination of observations, sketches, notes and quotes.' When George is in the field researching a story, she writes or sketches in her journal as part of her daily routine. As she takes research notes, records personal observations, and draws, her story line evolves" (67). I've included many examples of lessons that evolved from my notebook jottings in the chapters that follow.

My students will also learn the value of note taking throughout the year. My expectations for student notes are the same as for my own— they will use writing as a tool throughout the day to explore new learning, note interesting words, and record strategies being used for literacy learning. Much time will be spent during the first weeks of school helping students learn to use different notebooks for different purposes (see Figure 2.3). These logs will be stored on top of their desks, in open file boxes for each student, labeled for ready access.

A Change of Thought

My planning has changed over the last couple of years. I wanted to cut down on the amount of time I spent planning for word learning and the time my students lost for reading and writing while they completed word-learning activities. I was frustrated and overburdened developing lists and activities. I was also concerned about the amount of transfer that occurred as students memorized lists, completed activities, and played games. Each year many students were not able to generalize concepts from spelling lists to the point where they could use them in their reading and writing.

This past summer I reread notes and dusted off a couple of old textbooks as I attempted to revise my word study plans. While rereading from an old textbook, I came across an idea that I intuitively knew and trusted but that had been lost to curriculum mandates:

Formal instruction provides the basic knowledge; informal instruction teaches the skills, habits and understandings necessary for an independent mastery of the full vocabulary. . . .

The great bulk of words that children learn to spell are not learned from a spelling book at all. *They are learned as children write and read.* Accordingly, instructional time that is designated reading

Word Study Notebook
Students use this notebook during the word study block to

- Complete spelling activities
- Reflect on their learning about spelling
- Keep a personal word bank
- Write and monitor spelling goals

Inquiry Notebook
Students use this notebook during the science and social studies learning blocks to

- Take notes
- Write questions about curriculum content
- Use a variety of strategies for learning vocabulary
- Keep track of key content vocabulary
- Take notes while researching

Reading Notebook
Students use this notebook during daily read-aloud time to

- Develop reading comprehension strategies
- Make predictions
- Follow plot structure
- Keep track of characters
- Make connections
- Sketch
- Collect words
- Stretch their thinking about texts so that they can be involved in thoughtful conversations during the class read-aloud

Reading Log
Students have a folder in which they keep track of their independent reading. The reading log has a blank form that they use as a tool to help them understand their independent reading material. They use the log to

- State the purpose of their reading
- Make predictions
- Record their thoughts and questions
- Collect words

Writing Notebook
Students use this notebook to develop ideas for their writing drafts; they play with words and language in it. They use it as a prewriting tool across the school year.

Figure 2.3 The uses of student notebooks.

and language arts is also the time when the fruits of spelling instruction are harvested. Skilled teachers see to it that these activities are conducted so that vocabularies are expanded and correct spellings are learned. (Henderson 1990)

I now approach planning for word study differently. I think about the importance of short (ten- to fifteen-minute), explicit lessons. I also use read-aloud time to demonstrate, guide, and prompt students' thinking so that they will apply this thinking while independently reading and writing. Content area learning (math, social studies, and science) is rich with opportunities for me to teach or reinforce spelling and vocabulary strategies in a meaningful context, which is necessary for students as they demonstrate their understanding of the curriculum.

I've adopted the ritual of marking October 15 on my calendar, signaling the passage of six weeks of school. Consciously I work carefully toward this day. I know by this point in the school year my priority is forging a bond in which the students and I have built a trust in each other and the learning process. I want the students to have independent work habits so that I can begin flexible grouping for instruction as a means to support the group more effectively.

Now when I approach planning for the first six weeks of school, I segment my word-learning curriculum into three parts: word study block, read-aloud time, and vocabulary/content area instruction. These three curricular components guide me as I plan for word learning and the school day. I like to start my planning by thinking about the word study block and then branch out to read-aloud and content inquiries.

Word Study Block

The word study block is used for explicit instruction as I model, guide, and coach students as they form understandings about word-related concepts. Students work with words that exemplify conceptual knowledge relative to their demonstrated spelling knowledge.

The word study block begins with a short focus lesson crafted to draw students' attention to a spelling feature (vowel patterns, plurals, consonant doubling, spelling generalizations, using prefixes and suffixes). The focus lesson is a time for me to teach explicitly. "A good focus lesson has a very clear objective" (Ray and Laminack 2001). During the first six weeks of school I tell the students the name of the activity, why we are doing this particular activity, and where I see them applying this strategy or skill. I use the following framework for word study block.

Word Study Block
- Focus lesson
  Introduce activity
  Introduce concept
  Introduce word wall words
  Clarify observed confusions
- Word study activity
- Reflect/debrief

Students use notebooks during the word study block.

During the word study block, I create anchor charts to hold students' thinking or as a quick reference. Anchor charts are a visual way for me to introduce and demonstrate concepts to students. These charts are strategically posted around the room in different locations so that they are visible while students are working independently. The charts serve as a quick reference so that students do not lose momentum while writing or reading. On an anchor chart I try to include what is important in helping students understand concepts. The following types of anchor charts have helped my students develop an understanding of word study concepts.

Anchor Charts
- Spelling activities, including what, how, and why
- Spelling features web
- Editing thinking and strategies
- Capitalization chart, including why
- Parts of speech

I have found that by October most students come to the meeting area for the word study block with word study notebook in hand and ask the name of the activity so they can put the title at the top of a new page. This probably would not happen if students had not been introduced to the procedures, activities, and applications of a word study program.

Anchor chart for *their/there/they're.*

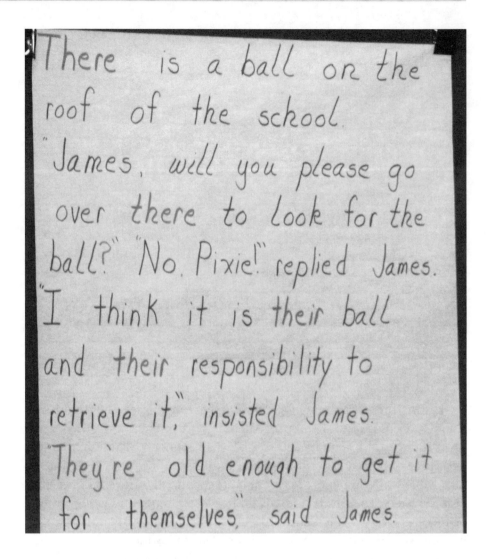

There is a ball on the roof of the school. "James, will you please go over there to look for the ball?" "No, Pixie!" replied James. "I think it is their ball and their responsibility to retrieve it," insisted James. "They're old enough to get it for themselves," said James.

Next, the children practice the skill or strategy in their word study notebook (subsequent chapters include many sample lessons from the word study block). We bring closure to the lesson with a brief reflection period. I have found that reflection has become a critical component in all units of the school day.

I ask students to reflect using one of the following questions:

What did you learn today?
How has this activity helped you as a reader or writer?
How do you see yourself using this word study learning while reading or writing?

Once I begin asking these questions, students' oral and written reflections help shape the focus for the next lessons. More important, I consider their

	Activity	**Purpose**
Week 1	Name explorations	Develop a common language to talk about words.
Week 2	Word observations	Create an eye for noticing print as students learn to look carefully across words.
Week 3	Word connections	Reinforce the generative concept of words—knowing a root word, syllable, or pattern, one can write another word or infer word meaning.
Week 4	Word sorts	Revisit how to categorize, classify, and store words by using sound, visual patterns, and meaning.
Week 5	Word webs	Create webs of words that have the same spelling feature. This builds on word sorts by emphasizing sound, visual patterns, and meaning of words.
Week 6	"Have a go"	Use spelling features of similar words to find and self-correct spelling errors.

Table 2.1 A Six-Week Plan for Word Study Block

comments in relation to their reading and writing performance, noting miscues and spelling confusions. These considerations help me to determine the content for future lessons.

Reflection is a time for me to bring closure to the day's lessons, by highlighting skill and strategy uses and having students share their learning. The sharing of different thinking and strategy use and application allows the group to grow as a learning community.

While planning for the first six weeks I map out a plan that allows me to go into depth as I help students become word-savvy (see Table 2.1). Over the years I have learned that it makes sense to revisit and build on how students look at print during the word study block. Students learn activities that they will use flexibly during the remainder of the school year. Word study notebooks are the primary tool for these activities.

Introductory lessons to use during the first six weeks of the word study block are included in Chapter 3, First Lessons.

Read-Aloud Time

I want my students to enjoy read-aloud time and look forward to it each day. Read-alouds are short and help students focus on words, especially the ones that we stop and discuss. During the first six weeks, I try to read aloud to my students four times a day (poetry, picture book, content material, and chapter book). I read aloud from many different texts prior to content area learning as a transition tool. I also read poetry to bring closure to the morning and school day.

I spend approximately thirty minutes reading aloud to my students after lunch while developing note-taking and conversation strategies. These read-aloud times help me apprentice my students to become thoughtful about their reading, thinking, note taking, and response to

Students sit in a circle and take notes while I read aloud Woodson's *The Other Side*.

texts, particularly the crafting of words. While reading I share my notes, thinking, and reflections from my notebook as I demonstrate and guide my students as they discover their own note-taking process.

I know that I am the type of person who reads with a pen in hand. I ask my students to read in similar ways. Students note or mark while reading. The students' notes and marks are an attempt to help them think about words and phrases while reading. I want to ensure that the daily reading (both independent and read-aloud) has an effect on their vocabulary growth.

Students learn the value of note taking during read-aloud, and then it becomes a tool adapted for myriad purposes. My goal is that by the beginning of November students are using note taking during most independent reading times.

During the first six weeks I read picture books during read-aloud, as students write in their notebooks. Picture books

- Do not take much planning time to read and reread
- Are well written, with great models of the language I am highlighting
- Help students develop listening and note-taking stamina
- Support students in learning to notice what I am highlighting
- Are easy to go back to and reread parts quickly as we revisit specific words and ideas

Brock and Cole read independently with their reading notebooks nearby.

• Are popular for independent reading as students develop their reading tastes and stamina

While investigating the layers of meaning that are in many picture books, I delve into the author's choice of words. My word study goal for the first six weeks is to support students as they become aware of words and how these words shape their images and thoughts.

Word Sketch and Stretch the Sketch are two activities I use to guide and coach the students at the beginning of the year during read-aloud time. For example, when reading Fletcher's *Twilight Comes Twice,* I share with the students how the author got me thinking as soon as I scanned the title:

I never thought about twilight happening twice each day. I only got a picture of that time right before sunset when everything is peaceful. I never thought of twilight during the morning when the sun rises. Now, each morning while I'm out for my morning run, lines from this book pop into my mind. The opening lines, "Twice each day a crack opens between night and day. Twice twilight slips through that crack," are lines that stick with me.

These are the kinds of thoughts I write in my notebook: "I like how Mr. Fletcher used an ordinary word like *crack* twice as he got me to reflect on twilight's moment." Today, while we are reading this book,

I want you to write words that paint an image in your mind. After you write the word down, try to sketch the picture in your mind's eye.

Michael asks, "So, let me get this straight. You want us to write and draw while you're reading?"

"Give it a try," I urge.

"Cool," Michael responds.

Kelsey interrupts, "You'd better read slowly."

Joseph wonders, "Should we find a word, one line, or all the lines that stick with us?"

"I want you to try and capture your thoughts and images of Ralph Fletcher's words," I say. "You tell me what works." I make an anchor chart to summarize read-aloud notebook recording.

Ideas to Record in Your Reading Notebook
- Thoughts or ideas the author got me to think about
- Words that stick out because they are new, interesting, or unusual, or I like the way they sound
- Lines that stick out because of the words or terms the author used
- Questions the author has made me wonder about
- A sketch that summarizes my thinking

Jackie thinks we should record only one word or line and, after the read-aloud, share thinking as a group. "I had something like that in mind, Jackie," I respond.

My goal is to stretch students' thinking as they key in on interesting words and phrases. I challenge them to create a sketch to help them think about the author's word choices and the images he creates for the reader.

As they converse about the books, the sketches help them develop an understanding of concepts and vocabulary. Once students are recording and sketching words, the next step is moving toward inferring word meaning. I ask the students to record their thinking as an assessment and conference tool for me. The students use their sketches and interesting words to confer with their reading partners or book clubs. These words then become words that are placed on the class word wall (see Chapter 7).

Figure 2.4 shows the page in Morgan's reading log on which she explored word use in *Twilight Comes Twice.* She considered the words and lines, trying to infer what Fletcher is getting the reader to think about. She wondered how he uses words selectively to create this image. Morgan's thinking about *luster* is a bit off track but does not affect her overall understanding of the text.

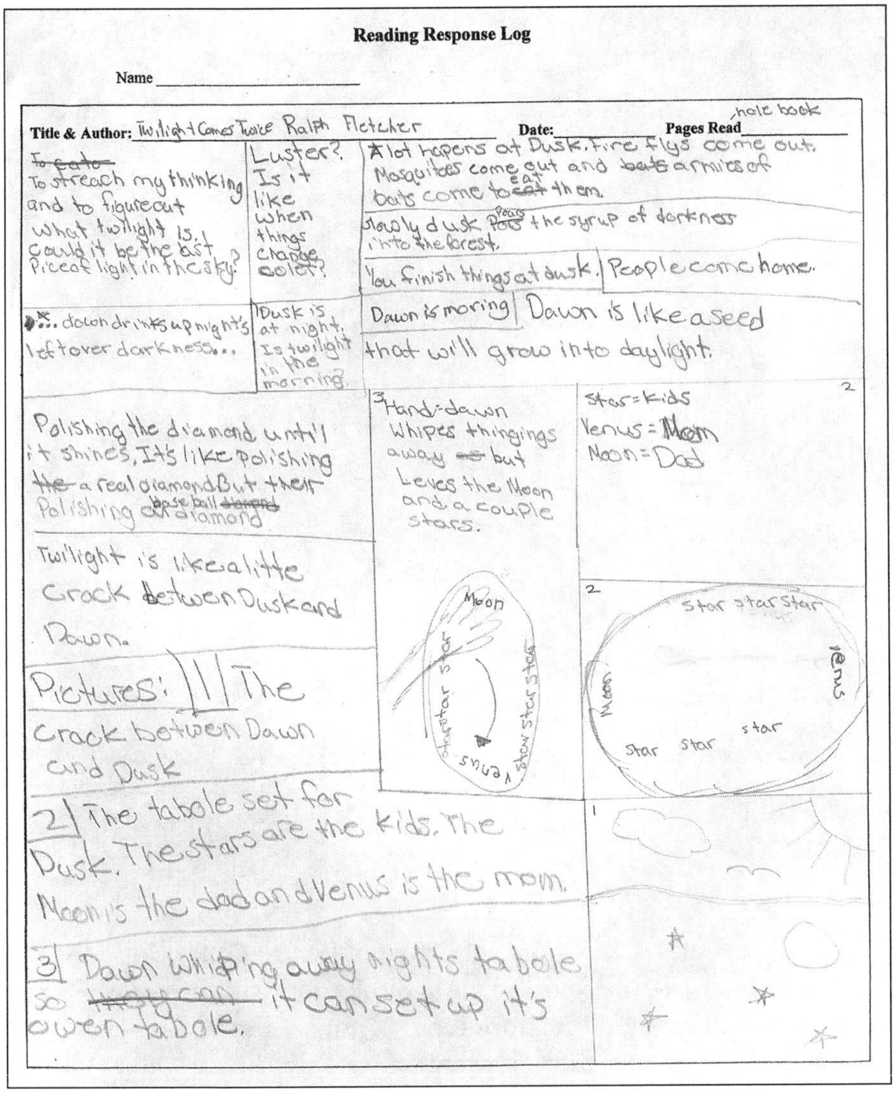

Reading Response Log

Name _____

Title & Author: Twilight Comes Twice Ralph Fletcher   Date: _____   Pages Read _____ hole book

To Get?
To streach my thinking and to figure out what twilight is. Could it be the last Piece of light in the sky?

Luster?
Is it like when things change color?

A lot hapens at Dusk. Fire flys come out. Mosquitoes come out and bats armies of bats come to EAT them.

slowly dusk Pours the syrup of darkness into the forest.

You finish things at dusk. People come home.

"... dawn drinks up night's leftover darkness..."

Dusk is at night. Is twilight in the morning.

Dawn is morning | Dawn is like a seed that will grow into daylight.

Polishing the diamond until it shines. It's like Polishing the a real diamond But their Polishing base ball diamond

3 Hand-dawn Whipes thingings away but Leves the Moon and a couple stars.

Star=Kids
Venus=Mom
Moon=Dad

Twilight is like a little crack between Dusk and Dawn.

Pictures: ||| The crack between Dawn and Dusk

2| The table set for Dusk. The stars are the kids. The Moon is the dad and Venus is the mom.

3| Dawn whiping away nights table so it can set up it's owen table.

Figure 2.4 Student's reading log page for Fletcher's *Twilight Comes Twice*.

Morgan has also organized her notebook using words along with sketches to explain complex ideas. She has a way to think about vocabulary to make sense of the text.

Lively read-aloud interactions grow out of demonstration, as students not only consider my thinking but begin to see how this can help them with their reading, writing, and thinking. So, as I search for picture books to read at the beginning of the year, I find my favorites (see Table 2.2).

They are my favorites because, first, I wish I could write like this. Second, I marvel over the author's word and language choices. I savor Cynthia Rylant's *In November*. She uses wonderful language, for instance, "In November, at winter's gate, the stars are brittle. The sun is a some-time friend. And the world has tucked her children in, with a kiss on their

	Goal	Notebook Task	Read-Aloud Books
Week 1	Listen to words.	Develop an ear for listening to words.	Fletcher, *Twilight Comes Twice*
Week 2	Note interesting words.	Record interesting words. Think about what makes them interesting.	Yolen, *Nocturne* Ray, *Basket Moon* London, *The Waterfall* Rylant, *An Angel for Solomon Singer*
Week 3	Note important words.	Record important words that help understanding of text. Think through the idea of interesting and important words.	Leavitt, *A Snow Story* Aliki, *Those Summers* Mochizuki, *Baseball Saved Us* Say, *Home of the Brave*
Week 4	Note words that create an image.	Record words that create an image.	Gray, *My Mama Had a Dancing Heart* Nikola-Lisa, *The Year with Grandma Moses* Burleigh, *Flight* Rylant, *In November*
Week 5	Word sketch.	For words that create an image, sketch the image. Think about how image and sketch help understanding of text.	Fletcher, *Hello, Harvest Moon* Pinkney, *Duke Ellington* Paulsen, *Canoe Days*
Week 6	Stretch the sketch.	Record and sketch images. Think about how image and sketch help stretch thinking about the text.	George, *To Climb a Waterfall* Horowitz, *Crab Moon* Woodson, *The Other Side* McDonald, *The Bone Keeper* Carlstrom, *Raven and River*

Table 2.2 A Six-Week Plan for Read-Aloud Word Learning

heads, till spring." Or the words of Gary Paulsen in *Canoe Days:* "Across water so quiet it becomes part of the sky, the canoe slides in green magic without a ripple." Or the intriguing "That summer the fence that stretched through our town seemed bigger" from *The Other Side* by Jacqueline Woodson.

Classroom conversations move from being in awe of words, to questioning words and wondering about words. Through it all, we are developing an environment where we write and talk about words, including our understandings and our questions. Table 2.2 outlines six weeks of read-aloud word learning.

Content Area Word Learning

Content area learning is ripe with opportunities to develop vocabulary skills. Each content area has a unique vocabulary. The sophistication of the material and its content is embedded in this language. Helping students develop strategies for learning these vocabularies is more than a

Students read an article from *Time for Kids,* highlighting titles and subtitles.

yearlong effort. I prioritize strategies and skills that intuition and experience have taught me students struggle with while learning content. I also limit myself to a few key goals connecting word and content learning. In my early weeks of planning for content area word learning, I focus on the following goals.

- Do students know when they do not know the meaning of a word or phrase?
- Do students know how to determine if a word or phrase is important for understanding the big ideas of a text?
- Do students have a strategy to figure out the meaning of an unknown word or phrase?
- Do students infer the meaning of unknown words?

I assist students in developing new strategies to tackle these issues as they read short texts during shared reading and eventually independent reading with coaching and guidance. Students need help as they use highlighters and pencils to identify unknown or important words and phrases.

I introduce vocabulary webs and other graphic aids as students develop tools that help them become strategic. These graphic aids help students synthesize what has been learned about syllables, root words, and affixes as they infer the meaning of new words.

Figure 2.5 Animal droppings word web.

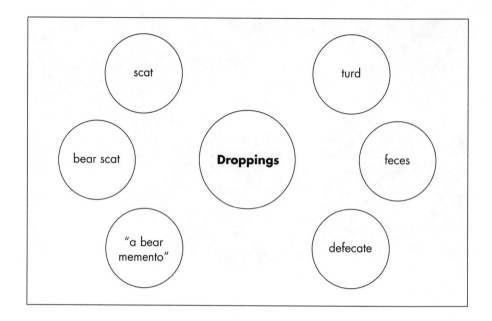

Some short nonfiction texts I use are

Write Time for Kids
Time for Kids—Exploring Nonfiction
Time for Kids Magazine
National Geographic for Kids
Bug Faces by Darlyne Murawski
Birds Build Nests by Yvonne Winer
A Drop of Water by Walter Wick
Plant Families by Carol Lerner
Going on a Whale Watch by Bruce McMillan
The Usborne Library of Science—Animal World

Find your own books, and share them with your students. Think carefully about what you want your students to learn about vocabulary through each text. Short texts work wonders for teaching or revisiting developing strategies and skills.

When I sit down to plan, I know that these short texts that take fifteen to twenty minutes to read in June take what feels like forever at the beginning of the year. This "forever" talk is necessary to help students see highlighting, underlining, and using graphic organizers as tools, not tasks. Students learn to respond to their reading by writing. I use shared writing to demonstrate how the students can use the text, their highlighted sections, or graphic organizers to add new vocabulary to their writing, demonstrating a growing awareness of topic and vocabulary.

	Goal	Notebook Task	Content Area Books
Week 1	Note unfamiliar words.	Record unfamiliar words.	Locker, *Water Dance* Locker, *Cloud Dance* "The Coral Reef Crisis"
Week 2	Note and infer word meanings.	Record unfamiliar words. Reread text as a strategy to infer meaning.	McMillan, *Going on a Whale Watch* (incl. Visual Glossary) Miller, *Arctic Lights, Arctic Nights* Siebert, *Mississippi*
Week 3	Note key words.	Record key words. Think about why these words are important in the text.	Gibbons, *The Moon Book* Furniss, *The Moon* Conrad, *Pedro's Journal* (could be used over a few weeks)
Week 4	Note related words.	Record related words. Infer the meaning of words by using related words in the text.	Swinburne, *The Woods Scientist* Montgomery, *The Snake Scientist* Borden, *America Is . . .*
Week 5	Use word webs.	Demonstrate how to use a word web of related words to infer the meaning of unfamiliar words.	Siy, *Footprints on the Moon* Yolen and Stemple, *Roanoke: The Lost Colony*
Week 6	Use linear arrays.	While reading a text, use a linear array to graphically represent understanding the meaning of a word.	Gibbons, *Planet Earth—Inside Out* Maestro and Maestro, *The New Americans* Nyquist, *Exploring Space*

Table 2.3 A Six-Week Plan for Content Area Word Learning

For example, my first science investigation involved trying to answer questions about food chains—exploring the idea of food webs and the concept that most animals' food comes from plants. I read Swinburne's *The Woods Scientist* to the class. This book describes understanding ecosystems by observation.

The vocabulary strategy I wanted students to develop was using context clues to determine the meaning of synonyms. This lesson fit in well with what we had been discussing because the students would have to determine what the synonyms are, use background information, and relate word meanings, similar to what we were doing during the word connections lessons in word study block. To help the students organize their thinking I used a semantic word web.

While reading, we came across some interesting information related to animal waste. The students enjoyed making a word web about it (see Figure 2.5). The conversation that supports making this type of word web has to be focused on why. Why are we making this web of words? How will this grouping help a reader understand the unknown words *feces, scat,* and *defecate,* and the phrase "a bear memento"? What background knowledge is used? Over the course of the week, I read aloud from other books that explore similar ideas. We added words to this list and created other word webs. Table 2.3 outlines six weeks of content area word learning.

Planning for word learning takes practice as I observe, analyze, and reflect about students' writing and reading processes. There is no short-cut to developing this craft.

First Lessons

*The very first thing I tell my new students on the first day of a
workshop is that good writing is about telling the truth. We are a
species that needs and wants to understand who we are.*

Anne Lamott (1994, 3)

The first day of school is never an easy walk in the woods. No
matter how thoroughly I have planned each moment, sur-
prises await. Students cross the threshold, jockeying for position in the classroom world. I allow them to select seats, then
write their names on adhesive name tags. While the students play musi-
cal chairs and explore the classroom library, I roam around the room,
learning names, collecting student paper trails, picking up a morsel of
information about a child or two, bonding.

I look forward to the beginning of each new school year as I learn
about the students in my class. I try to follow Don Graves's advice from
Bring Life into Learning: "Bypass people and you bypass learning." These
first few days' impressions set the tone for learning for the remainder of
the school year, as the students and I bond. I want the students to know
me as a mentor, teacher, learner, coach, but most important, as a trust-
worthy adult. We spend what seems like an inordinate amount of time
sitting in a circle listening to each other—learning nicknames, habits,
likes, dislikes, who is tentative, who likes to be in the spotlight. Most of
all, we develop a trust for each other—a learning community.

The first few weeks of word-learning activities build an understanding
of words as well as a vocabulary for discussing words and word-learning
procedures. Beginning with the first day's activity, I record anecdotal notes
that help me learn about my students and their spelling knowledge.

My goals for the first month's word learning are to

- Create an interest in words (play, laugh, think about words)
- Conduct name activities (look carefully at names, sort and resort
  names, investigate name origins)
- Develop a common vocabulary for talking about words
  (consonants, vowels, syllables, root words, prefixes, suffixes)
- Assess individual students informally to learn about their decoding,
  spelling, and vocabulary strategies
- Introduce a framework for studying and investigating spelling
  features
- Introduce core word study activities that will be used during
  investigations of spelling features
- Introduce the word study notebook (support understanding of how
  to use it as a tool for learning)

- Use "lines that stick with me" from books, newspapers, magazines, billboards, songs, or conversations to build word-learning community

Name Explorations (Week 1)

I bring my class of fifth graders to a circle with an anxious feeling in my stomach. The children have returned to the meeting area from their first look at the classroom library. Joseph remarks how excited he is to see mystery books and shows Osborne's *Spider Kane and the Mystery Under the May-Apple* as he shares the contents of the back jacket.

Kelsey interrupts to ask me if I have any Harry Potter books—she did not see any on the shelves. Before I can respond, she blurts, "I tried reading the first one this summer but just couldn't get into it. I saw the movie and thought I might give it another chance." This is my first observation of Kelsey asking and then answering her own questions, a pattern that will be repeated throughout the year. I respond, "It took me a while to get into Harry Potter. I've only read the first one myself. Once I got the characters straightened out and got used to the writing style, I had a hard time putting it down."

The class begins to fidget as I tell them how hard studying words was for me: "I used to read words and not pay that much attention to how they sounded, what they looked like, or what they meant. When I wrote, I wasn't thoughtful about the words I chose to use." Melissa, who had patiently kept her arm raised, whispers, "That's me, too." Side conversations erupt as other children share similar stories.

I continue my talk: "Then I began writing. This helped me think about my own words and the words I read. Now I'm hooked on thinking about words." I show the students a page from my writing notebook on which I've pasted and played with words from a newspaper (see excerpt in Figure 3.1).

I like to show this page to my students because I found an unusual word with a pronunciation guide, *Pilates,* and played with the pronunciation. I also goofed around with dialogue, using the phrase, "Yes, sir." This is one way I envision my class playing with words daily. The group seems excited about the thought of keeping their own notebooks.

I forget basic management somewhere in the heat of this August day, and the lesson begins to drag on, filled with too much teacher talk. I'm not sure how the students are going to relate to the first day's planned activity. Is this too basic? This group seems sophisticated—will this insult their intelligence? Do they really need a model? What will they think of my model?

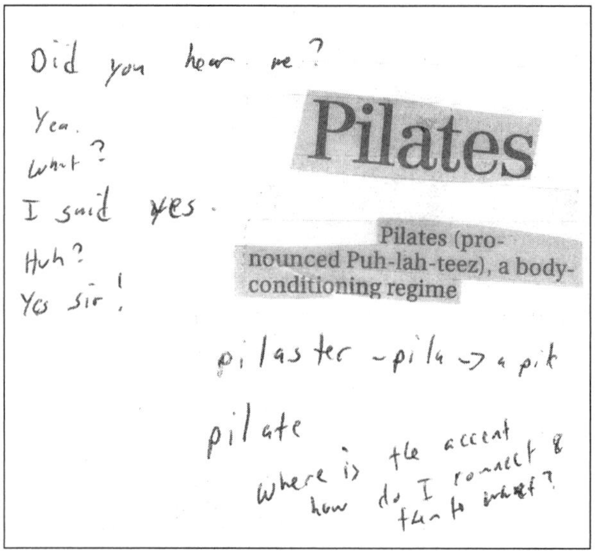

Figure 3.1 *Pilates* page from my notebook.

These questions and a dozen others race through my mind as I continue explaining the year's word-learning plans. I tell the kids, "We are going to study words differently. We will have short lessons that will help you understand yourselves as spellers while learning how to spell. We will not have spelling lists, but I will test you in other ways."

This is met by a chorus of cheers. I finish the introduction by adding, "Today's lesson and the lessons for the rest of the week will focus on looking at our names."

The first word study lessons are used to build a common language to talk about words over the course of the school year. I like to use the students' first names to help build this common vocabulary. Their first names are displayed, observed, sorted, and discussed as I help students understand the complex relationship of sound, pattern, and meaning.

Vowel patterns, syllables, and root words found in the students' names will be highlighted during the first week's lessons. I want these first lessons to anchor word learning and to develop a community of word-sensitive learners. Students become comfortable interacting with each other as they learn to listen and respond to their classmates and me.

I can see some students looking around, trying to escape the circle, as I begin to explain the first names activity. I quickly regroup by pulling out a 4" x 6" index card with my name thoughtfully drawn out (see Figure 3.2). I explain what I tried to do with my name using limited artistic ability.

I explain how I worked in my three sons and my wife because family is important to me. I've used purple because it is my favorite color. I quickly ask the circled group what they think they will put on their cards.

Figure 3.2 "Max" drawing.

I'm met by a dumbfounded silence. Kelsey breaks the silence by announcing, "I want to highlight my love for shopping, reading, and the Buckeyes." I hand her an index card, tell her to give it a go. Brad states, "I want to include soccer and the Columbus Crew in mine." Other students blurt out a variety of ideas.

I distribute the remainder of the index cards, eager to see what the students will accomplish. They get to work, comparing index cards as they converse about their name designs. I learn that I have a chatty bunch.

Chris is deliberate as he watches his peers and begins. There is thoughtfulness to Chris's work. He is the kid who hesitated at the door. When he did enter, he wouldn't remove his sideways ball cap or black bike glove. After twenty short minutes of watching students' work habits, conferring with kids, and focusing my thinking, we reconvene. We once again make a circle where students can see and talk with one another.

This short activity time has provided me with an opportunity to get a first impression of individual work habits, who works with whom (no assigned seats yet). I put names to faces and learn a bit about some individual students. My brief interactions during this lesson and the next few days' lessons help me build a trust with Chris, Jackie, Skye, and many other students that allows me to push their thinking, and especially their writing.

The reflection part of the lesson begins with me collecting the students' index card names and displaying them in three groups on the wall. Figure 3.3 shows an example of this idea. The students begin to read the names as I put them up. "You're putting the most colorful over here." "No, no!" interrupts Michael, "the size of the letters and the names." I continue to put them up, and Morgan adds to the conversation, "There is something about the vowels."

This prompts Laura and Kelsey to challenge me. "We think Emily and Jessica need to be in the third column because you are sorting the words by syllable." We all stop, ponder the statement by reviewing the

Figure 3.3 Students' name drawings. Students use their name drawings to let me and the class learn who they are.

names in each column, and then agree to move Jessica and Emily from the second column into the third.

I ask Laura and Kelsey how they knew I was sorting the names by syllable. "Morgan got us thinking when she asked about vowels. We noticed that each syllable has a vowel." Steven bravely asks, "Does each syllable have a vowel?" We go back and read each name, stressing syllables. We generalize that each syllable does have a vowel (something I assumed fifth graders already understood).

These contributions illustrate the type of conditions that need to be present for honest inquiry and discussion. The circle is important for students to learn to listen and respond to their peers.

Sometimes peers carry the conversation further; other times, they stop the conversation for clarification or questions. Still other times, an individual or a group of students may steer the conversation in a new direction based on connections made.

Learners need to be responsible for their learning. "Teachers can guide learners, but the learner must do the learning" (Bean and Bouffler 1997). Later on, I read *Table Manners* by Radunsky. Since the book is written in dialogue form, on the title page there is an interesting thought: "What you need is . . . Table Manners . . . The edifying story of two friends whose discovery of good manners promises them a glorious future."

I go back and reread the part that begins with "The edifying" while wondering out loud what *edifying* means. Dumbstruck that the teacher is baffled, the students are silent for an uncomfortable moment. Taking advantage of the silence, I ask, "How could I figure out what *edifying* means?" Dan suggests, "You could get a dictionary to look it up." Josh, whose hand shot up when he heard the word *dictionary,* volunteers to retrieve a dictionary and look it up for the group. I ask Josh how the dictionary will help. "It will tell us what the word means. It will give us definitions," he proudly responds. "What if I can't understand the definition?" I challenge Josh. Brad rescues Josh, "You could ask the teacher."

Pausing again, I wonder if there will be any more suggestions, but there aren't (must be a first-day thing). I learn about the inner workings of a dictionary after this question, but more important, I learn about my students and their understanding of vocabulary strategies or what they think I want to hear.

I do not retrieve a dictionary, nor do I continue trying to define *edifying* at this time. My focus for the read-aloud is helping students understand how to interact as part of our classroom community.

I will take the time during the second reading of *Table Manners* to teach the vocabulary strategy of using context as a means to infer word meaning. This is an instance of planting a seed of thought that I will use in the future with a specific agenda. The question still in the back of my mind, and one I want to get in the back of the students' minds is, What is the importance of this word in understanding this text?

I choose *Table Manners* as the first read-aloud of the school year so that the students and I can begin discussing what classroom conversation manners look, sound, and feel like. I ask that they refrain from raising their hands to share their ideas throughout the year. This is a tough habit for many students to break. They have learned to play the question/answer game well. The first weeks of school are filled with conversations about how to have a dialogue in which the students' opinions, thoughts, and visions are welcome.

I have come to view our classroom dialogue as comprising thoughtful conversations. I know with three boys and a working wife, our dinner table conversation would get confusing if we were not able to face each other. Looking at the speaker is a courtesy that I want my students to adopt. I have reconfigured my room over the years so that there is a large meeting area in the classroom where the group can sit at eye level (including me) in a circle.

Dinner table chat helps as a metaphor in developing a rapport where the expectation is to talk without raising hands, listen to each other carefully, and then respond. This is a skill that takes time, demonstration, guidance, and coaching.

I do not want to simplify the complexity of language development; instead I want to support students as they grow in their awareness and use of oral and written language. I want to accomplish this by creating a classroom that replicates the conditions found during an apprenticeship. In creating the classroom community it is important to have conditions that support inquiry, rigor, feedback, analysis, and discussion.

The first day spins by. Word study block was wedged between reading workshop and writing workshop. The notebook was handy but felt awkward. My notebook scribbles are barely legible, although organized in one place.

I read what I have written. *Joseph*—written next to his name are the descriptors *thoughtful, artistic, respectful. Jackie*—I have jotted the following thoughts: "mixes caps, lowercase, Jackie with an E, laughs, sits on edge [between boys and girls]." Next to *Dan* is written "Mr. Baseball." Then there is *Skye.* I did not have time to write anything about her as I was observing the students, but now I take a moment to write some thoughts: "She worked by herself and constantly came up to me for positive reinforcement and a new direction." I reexamined her name as it hung on the wall (see Figure 3.4) and added "mixes caps with lowercase, all caps, *day's/days, rasing/racing,* she traced over her pencil work, colorful, and she loves racing cars." I pack my notebook in my unusually light sack as I head out the door.

Word study had been slipped into the first day's lesson plan rather than waiting, as it previously had, until I had formally assessed each child. I have discovered that my informal observations, and student comments and reflections, provide me with more valuable information than I would have paid attention to from the formal assessment.

The rest of this short first week (only Thursday and Friday) is spent revisiting the name chart and recording target words and observations in word study notebooks.

Figure 3.4 Skye's name drawing.

Word Study Notebooks

Word study notebooks are at the heart of the word study curriculum, and [illegible] t weeks of school making the use of [illegible] ıup how I use my notebook as a con- [illegible] rpts from texts. I talk to the group [illegible] ernoons and pulling *Sports Illustrated* [illegible] ın article or two before my children [illegible] ınusual word that I had not come [illegible]

[illegible] g of a time it will come out either in [illegible] ıy write. I say, "This is your warning. [illegible] run into an unusual word." I also [illegible] evious year so they can understand [illegible] t.

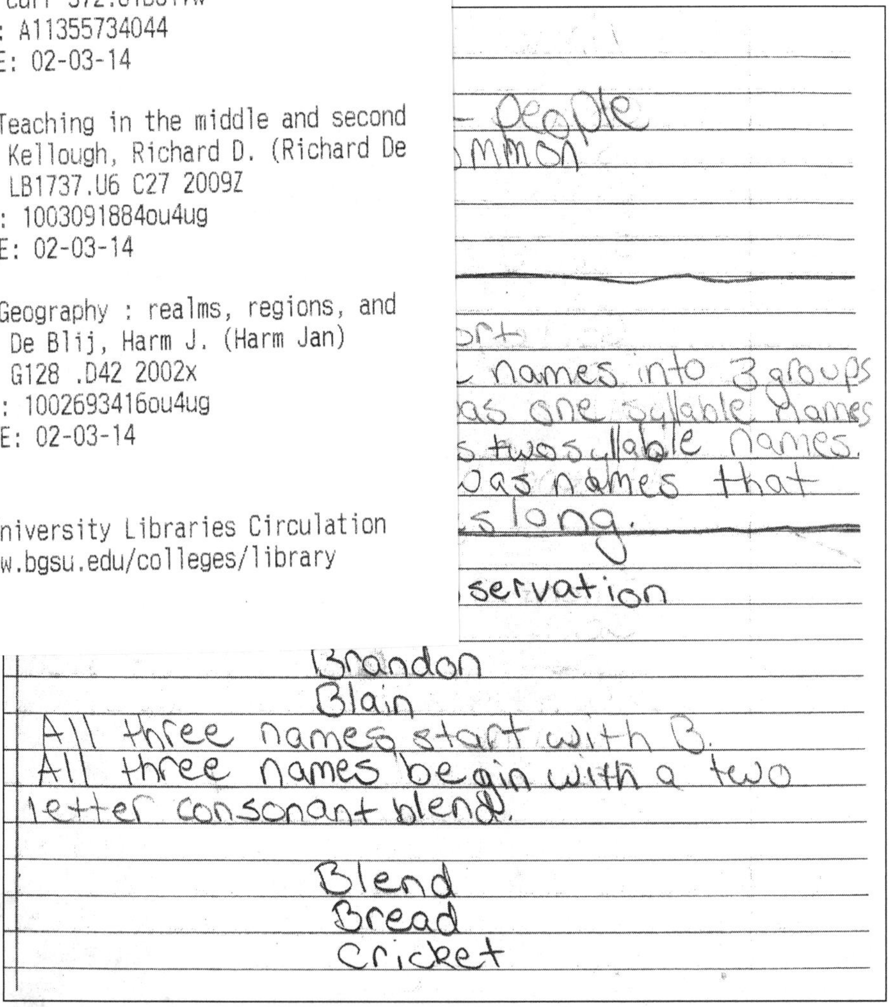

Student's word study notebook entry.

Brad interrupts my demonstration by challenging me: "I get it—we'll have a fancy place to do spelling." Then I pause. I let it roll off my shoulders. Trina trips Brad up by interjecting, "It sounds like a whole lot of work, if you ask me." (I realize she is not quite to the point of mastering her table manners yet.) To help dispel confusion, I move the demonstration to think-aloud.

I show the class my notebook, thumbing through its pages. I demonstrate on a piece of chart paper (with a little of their help) what I expect from a notebook entry.

I am a little disappointed as I walk around the room observing the first entries. The notebook entries are regurgitated summaries of what I had modeled and discussed. This did help build a strong foundation for group discussion, one of this class's pleasures and strengths. I discovered that the class did take away the big ideas from the talk, and I got some interesting spellings for *syllable*.

Introducing Vocabulary Instruction

During the third day of school I like to begin vocabulary instruction. My focus for the first few weeks will be helping students learn to determine important words, and why students think they are important. I use short texts that I have collected over the years. (*Time for Kids—Exploring Nonfiction* is my favorite.)

"The Coral Reef Crisis" (from the *Time for Kids—Exploring Nonfiction* kit) is a text I like to use early in the year. This text has proved to hold students' interest, and includes a variety of text features and interesting vocabulary. This lesson provides me with a good piece of baseline data as I begin to assess students' vocabulary understanding.

Students read the text and use highlighters to mark words they think are important. While they are reading, I move around the room noting words highlighted and chatting with the kids. I want to get a feel for their thinking. Students often highlight a large portion of the text. I ask them to highlight no more than five words, but this does not prevent an abundance of highlights on many students' texts.

I use shared or choral reading to reread the text. I have an overhead copy of the text, so that the group can reread the text and observe my demonstration. When I feel the majority of students have finished reading and highlighting the text, I call their attention to the overhead screen and ask them to read along with me.

I read the title, subtitle, and captions at the top of the page. I highlight the word *crisis* from the title and tell the group that this word will guide my thinking as I read the remainder of the article. I continue my demonstration by highlighting the words *people, pollution,* and *warming* from the subtitle. As I pause to scan the group, Morgan says, "I highlighted *danger.*" A majority of the class nods in approval of Morgan's thinking.

I wonder aloud, "How does danger go with the idea of crisis?" This brings a moment of reflective silence. Joseph breaks the silence: "I think the subtitle should all be underlined because it helps me think a lot about the coral reef crisis." We agree that it is hard to highlight only individual words, especially in titles and headings.

Dan returns the group's thinking to selecting individual words by stating, "Well, if we can only highlight words, then *crisis* and *danger* work for me." We continue to move through the article, trying to decide important words. Agreement does not come easily to this group, so we use consensus to settle disputes and begin agreeing that there may be more than one correct response.

I use demonstration to support students' thinking, showing the students that my text has only a few words highlighted. Jaws drop; many of the students had marked up most of their text.

I explain why I highlighted the word *crisis* and words related to the crisis: "*Crisis* helped me focus my thinking on what I thought was the main idea of this passage." I see lots of head nodding. Tyler wants to know if we can do this again. Brad adds that it was sort of fun once I showed them how. Abby hesitantly admits this was hard to do. I'm finding that my students like support and guidance. We are beginning to meld as a community of learners interested in everyone's thinking, including the how and why of words.

First Week Goals Accomplished
- Introduced a word study lesson format.
- Established a ritual of talking about words.
- Created an interest in words.
- Created an interest in a word study notebook.
- Started developing a language to talk about words.
- Introduced the idea of an open sort.
- Introduced the idea of reflecting in a word study notebook.

Word Observations (Week 2)

The word observations activity is one I like to introduce and use during the second week of school. Word observations are designed to help students focus their attention on salient features of words (e.g., adding affixes or consonant doubling). Students learn to look for patterns and features that are unique to the feature being studied. They will be guided to observe, note, and monitor their use of these features while reading and writing. My goal is to guide students to think about important features of words that often get neglected in traditional spelling memorization activities. Word observations are a core activity that students will use as a learning tool in the classroom; ideally this will become a tool they use beyond the classroom.

Observation is a skill that students use across the curriculum, so word study is no different. Students learn to anticipate the powerful but overused question, "What do you notice?"

By this point, I have had time to read with each student and take notes about the group's spelling needs; I think about the type of words to use for the first word observation activity. High-frequency words like *maybe, finally,* and *used* are typically misspelled by many students. These words have proved helpful in introducing word observations to my students in the past. Since I use words that are commonly misspelled, these words support the type of talk that I want my students to develop during word observations.

If you think these words are too basic for fifth graders, you are right. Yet each year I have students who need this support. These error patterns are sometimes difficult to get under control because the children have been practicing these habits for a long time.

I also need to be clear with students about the purpose of the activity, which is teaching them where and how to look so that they can monitor their own misspellings.

Making Choices for Word Observation

Sound	*Pattern*	*Meaning*
High-frequency words	Doubled consonant as part of root word	Root words
Short vowels	Consonant doubling when adding suffix	Affixes
Long vowels	Stressed and unstressed syllables and effect on vowel patterns	Word origins
	Dropping *e* to add suffix	Homophones and homographs
	Use knowledge of single-syllable words	

The first word observation lesson is a demonstration lesson. This demonstration is designed to allow the students to know what word observations sound and feel like as well as what will be expected of them during the lesson. The children are finishing their independent reading, recording thoughts in their reading logs, and trying to figure out what is next. I invite them to bring their word study notebooks to the easel area.

"Today we are going to do a new activity, called word observations. Word observations will help you look closely at spelling features in words." I write "Word Observations" and the day's date at the top of a piece of chart paper. "Please turn to a clean page in your word study notebook and copy this heading," I direct the group. As the students are copying from the chart, I remind them to use their best handwriting. Word study provides a good opportunity to work on handwriting and correct letter formation. Copying individual words during the observations goes a long way toward helping students use spelling features in their everyday writing.

Word Observation
maybe
- Compound word *may* and *be*
- Two syllables *may/be, may · be*
- Question type of word
- Long vowels
- Five-letter word

I have decided to use the word *maybe* for the first word observation because many of the students have misspelled this word. While I am writing *maybe* on the chart, I ask the students to watch how I write it. Once the word is on the chart, Katie asks, "Should we write it in our notebook?" I respond, "Write *maybe* in your notebook using your neatest handwriting. While you are writing, think about what you know about *maybe*." The students begin copying. I make sure I notice how Jackie and Brad copy from the chart because I have discovered they often spell *maybe* as *mybe* and do not copy well from resources.

The demonstration moves on. I tell the group that what I notice about the word *maybe* is that it is a compound word. Chris adds, "It has two syllables." I write "compound word" and "two syllables" on the chart under *maybe*. I continue writing and talking: "*Maybe* has a long vowel in the first and in the last syllable." The students copy my writing from the chart. Nick informs the group, "The syllable break is where the two words connect."

Jackie adds, "I keep forgetting that *a*." I respond, "I know that when I write words I write all the time I may forget a letter because my mind is on the next word. It is important that when you reread your writing, you pay attention to words where you may have forgotten a letter because of writing quickly. This is what word observation will help you do." This lesson lasts about ten minutes but builds on the work with syllables from last week and the importance of rereading one's writing that I continually stress with the group.

Word observations not only help students learn how to look at words and develop a vocabulary to talk about words. The focus words also become words that students learn to spell correctly. Word observations help students develop monitoring skills as they learn to detect their own errors. This process is slow at the beginning of the year but soon gets integrated into the students' thinking. Melissa, who spelled *said/sead,* and Morgan, who spelled *also/alsow,* learned through word observations how to find their mistakes and not continue making the same spelling error over and over.

I remind them of the baby steps we take while learning something new. By the end of the week I have the students observe words like *disappear* or *collection.* I like to use these words because the root words have doubled consonants along with a prefix and a suffix. *Doubled consonants, prefix,* and *suffix* become part of the vocabulary that students use as we discuss spelling and vocabulary by noticing word parts. I have used the following words during the first weeks of the word observations activity and throughout the year. These are words that have worked for me over the years. I try to pick words that allow me to discuss many spelling features. The most helpful resource is the students' writing and the spelling features they are not attending to.

Word Observations List

High-Frequency Words	Compound Words	Doubled Consonants
again	*maybe*	*huddle*
know	*everybody*	*pollute*
until	*notebook*	*success*
very	*basketball*	
about	*anyone*	

Vowel Patterns	Plurals	Affixes
complain	*fields*	*usually*
exceed	*voices*	*finally*
survive	*atlases*	*preview*
resume	*cities*	*foresee*
thirsty	*passes*	*successful*
turtle		*quietest*

The class creates an anchor chart by the end of the week summarizing the word observation task (see Figure 3.5). I use my planning notebook notes with shared writing to create similar anchor charts for word learning throughout the year. The first sentence is typically a task description of what the students do, and why.

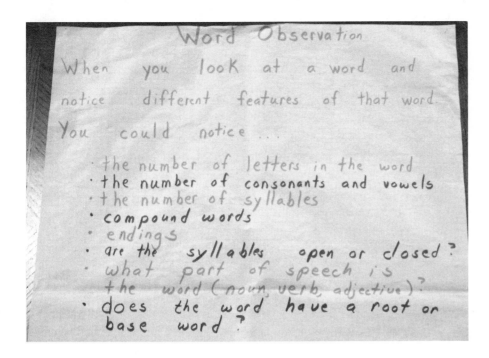

When you look at a word and notice different features of that word. You could notice...

- the number of letters in the word
- the number of consonants and vowels
- the number of syllables
- compound words
- endings
- are the syllables open or closed?
- what part of speech is the word (noun, verb, adjective)?
- does the word have a root or base word?

Figure 3.5 Anchor chart created by the class at the end of first week of word observation.

Second Week Goals Accomplished

Students learn to

- Notice and think about words
- Monitor misspellings by rereading their own writing
- Know where to look for their own misspellings
- Note their own error patterns
- Identify example words to help them spell unknown words that fit the same spelling feature

Word Connections (Week 3)

The third week's lessons build on previous lessons. I ask students to make connections to what they know as they write unknown words. Building vocabulary and concept development take time, repetition, and use in a meaningful context. I try to make the context meaningful by using a word that I noticed many of my students misspelling. Content area investigations are a great resource for finding words that a majority of students use and have difficulty spelling (see Chapter 6).

While collecting words in my notebook, I record the students' names and their misspellings. I then group these misspellings by similar spelling errors. This gives me a snapshot of spelling strategies students are using. By the end of Week 3, I know *exploration* will be a good word for introducing the word connections activity.

Anchor chart for word connections, emphasizing ways to connect spelling features to more than one word.

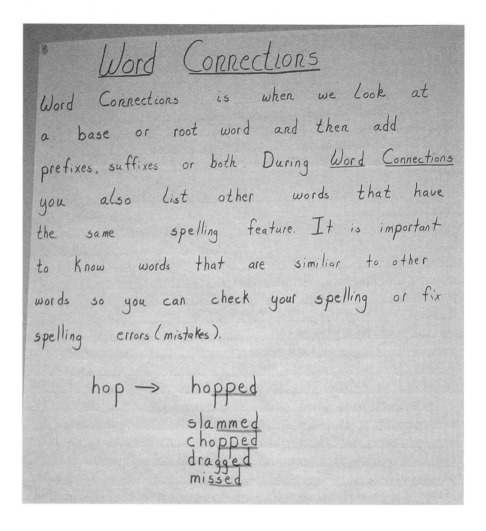

Word Connections

Word Connections is when we look at a base or root word and then add prefixes, suffixes or both. During Word Connections you also list other words that have the same spelling feature. It is important to know words that are similar to other words so you can check your spelling or fix spelling errors (mistakes).

hop → hopped

slammed
chopped
dragged
missed

"Please open to a clean page in your word study notebook. Today we are going to do a new activity. We will use what we know about root words and suffixes to help us spell *exploration*," I tell the students.

Morgan, speaking over the page turning, asks, "What should we call this?" "Word connections," I respond and then write it at the top of the chart paper. The lesson continues with me thinking out loud: "What do I know about *exploration*?" A pause leaves enough time for Tyler to use his developing table manners and suggest, "Three syllables." Skye challenges him, "I think there are four syllables." Michael tries to settle the disagreement by clapping out the syllables as he says, "Exploration."

The group agrees with Skye. I acknowledge Tyler's thinking as Kelsey adds, "*Explore* is the first part of the word." I write *explore* on the chart. Most of the students copy it into their word study notebooks. I quickly scan the room to locate Jackie, Brad, Melissa, and Nick, making sure they have copied *explore* correctly from the chart.

Students share with each other before reporting what they learned to the whole class.

"What's next?" I inquire. "It sounds like you need to add an *a,*" Matt answers. J.J. adds, "You need to drop the *e* before adding the *a.*" I write what both boys said on the chart. Matt looks at the chart and grins while agreeing with J.J.

I cross out Matt's suggestion, but make the point that "we need to balance what sounds right with what looks right"—another prompt that will help students use visual analysis. Wondering if Jackie remembers Friday's lesson, I ask her, "What suffix do we add in *exploration*?" She looks back at Friday's lesson and the ending of *collection.* "*t, i, o, n,*" she announces. I write *exploration* under the previous chart entries.

I wrap up the lesson by asking the students to take a moment to write what they learned in their word study notebooks. I move around the group, touching base with Nick, Abby, and Drake. They were quiet and seated toward the back. Drake informs me he has misspelled *exploration* the last couple of days. I let him know that he isn't the only one.

The students share with a partner instead of with the group. This saves time and gives me an opportunity to listen in on students' explanations. I reiterate points I heard made between partners to the whole group: "If you know how many syllables, it helps you think about each word part" and "You need to remember to look and see if the word looks like it is spelled right." I add that it was great how we used what we had learned in the past two weeks. I mention that I like how Jackie looked back in her word study notebook to help her connect the suffix. Praise needs to be specific, especially when I try to reinforce behaviors I value.

Third Week Goals Accomplished
Students learn to
- Use what they know about a word to spell an unknown word
- Visually monitor spelling of unknown words
- Regularly use the word study notebook as a tool to think about words
- Think through spelling features when attempting to spell unknown words

Word Sorts (Week 4)

It is now the fourth week of school, and the children have developed the habit of coming over to the easel area with their word study notebooks as we reflect on reading workshop and then move into the daily word study lesson. The students are growing in their use of the word study vocabulary, which they will use this week as they sort words into categories.

Brad asks, "What are we doing today?" I inform the group, "Today we are going to do a word sort." Laura tells me, "I've done this before." I ask Laura and the rest of the group, "Have you ever done an open sort?" Laura's questioning look lets me know that I probably will need to demonstrate more than I thought.

I show the students the twelve words written on the chart:

plugged	*missed*	*cheered*	*flutter*
raced	*chewed*	*rabbit*	*owed*
spelled	*dragged*	*gossip*	*cared*

I tell the group that I am scanning the list, observing different spelling features. While scanning the list, I am looking for key words. These key words will help me while I am sorting words into groups of words with similar spelling features. When doing an open sort, I try to have a group of words that could be sorted in more than one way. I am always curious to know how students are looking at words and then categorizing them.

The first word I choose is *plugged*. I write it down on another piece of chart paper. I am looking for words that have the same spelling feature as *plugged*. Abby interrupts my thinking with, "And what feature would that be?" Joseph answers for me, "Words that have double consonants." "No, there has to be something else. Too many words have double consonants," Abby responds.

Student's word sort.

Word Sort		
plugged	Flutter	Chewed
	rabbit	cheered
spelled	gossip	raced
dragged	My rule	owed
missed	is they have	cared
	to have double	
My rule	consants.	My rule
is they have		is they
to have two		have to end
over the same		them in a single
no letter and		consedent then
they have to		added.
end it with		
ed.		

"You're right, Abby, there is something more to this group than double consonants. I was putting words into this group where you need to double the consonant before adding -*ed*." Michael interjects, "Then the list should be *plugged, missed, spelled,* and *dragged.*"

"Maybe" is my response—a way of getting the group to take a closer look at the list. Morgan announces, "*Spelled* doesn't work. It already has a double consonant in the root word." Michael, starting to see the pattern, says, "Hey, *missed* doesn't work either." I cross out both words from the list, and we finish the sort having three categories—adding -*ed,* doubled consonant in root word, and doubling the consonant to add –*ed.*

Brandon remarks that he learned to look closely by sorting words. He has to be careful with consonant doubling in his writing. Consonant doubling and adding -*ed* or -*ing* is the area in which he made most of his spelling errors in his turtle research draft that he had finished editing that morning (see Figure 3.6).

I try to follow the kids' lead about what spelling features they are not attending to while writing daily. We had just finished drafting, revising, and editing research reports about our class turtle. The lesson of when to double the consonant was ignored or forgotten in many students' writing. Teaching a lesson once is not enough, especially with a challenging

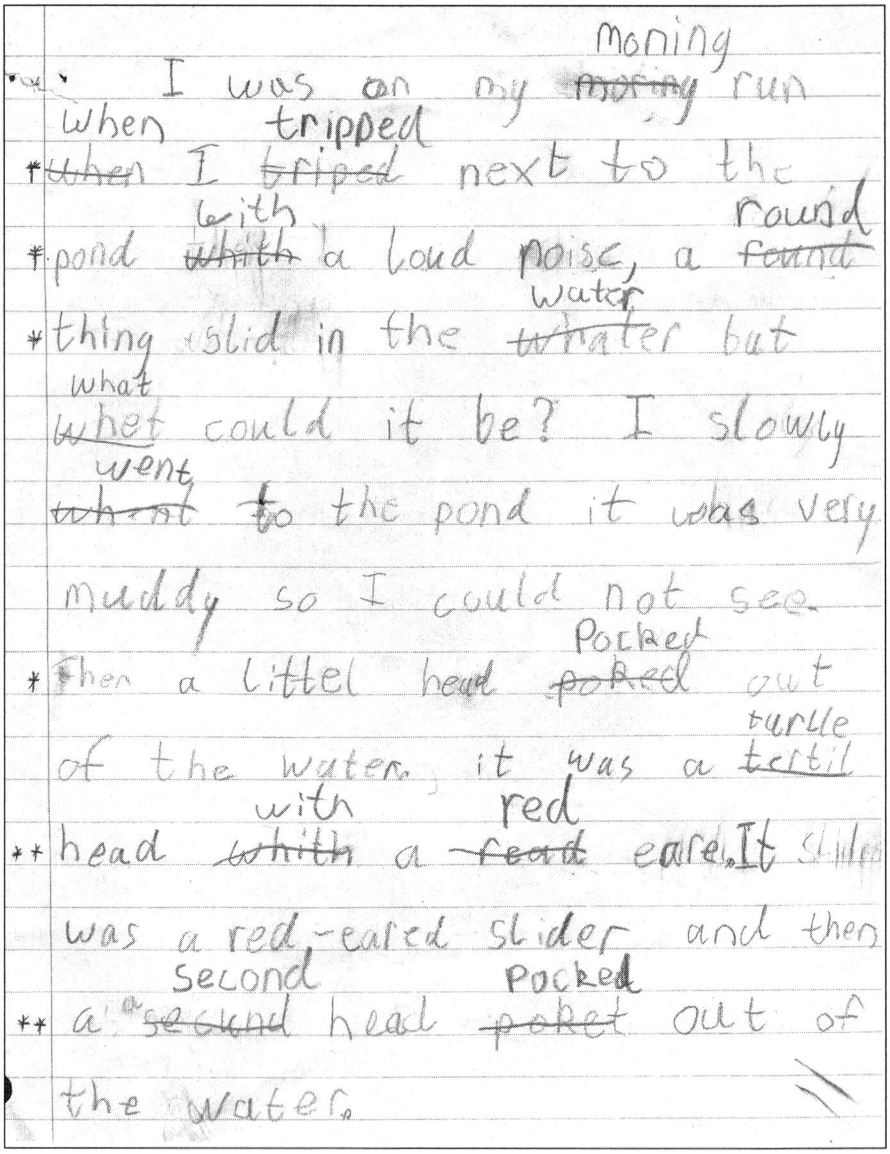

Figure 3.6 A page from student's draft of turtle report, edited to correct spelling.

I was on my ~~morny~~ moning run ~~when~~ when I ~~triped~~ tripped next to the ~~pond~~ with a loud noise, a ~~fornd~~ round thing slid in the ~~wtrater~~ water but ~~whet~~ what could it be? I slowly ~~whent~~ went to the pond it was very muddy so I could not see. ~~Then~~ a ~~littel~~ head ~~poked~~ Pocked out of the water, it was a ~~tertil~~ turtle ~~with~~ head ~~whith~~ a ~~fead~~ red ~~eare.~~ eare. It slid was a red-eared slider and then a ~~sesund~~ second head ~~poket~~ Pocked out of the water.

spelling feature like consonant doubling. My goal is to get students to look closely at print. Word sorts help students accomplish this. I ask the students to reflect in writing about how they are sorting words.

Fourth Week Goals Accomplished
Students learn to
- Categorize words by using spelling features
- Use words with the same spelling features to spell an unknown word
- Regularly monitor their own misspellings
- Regularly note their own error patterns

- Continue to identify example words to help them spell unknown words that fit the same spelling feature
- Use the word study notebook as a tool to reflect about spelling features

The first few weeks of school are methodically planned. I want to ensure that my students have adequate time to learn the routines and basic word activities that I will use throughout the year. I also want to give them time to develop and use appropriate vocabulary for thinking about, discussing, and reflecting on words.

My goal at the end of this time is for students to write their own spelling goals (see Chapter 4). By the end of the year, I want my students to reflect like Drake, "At the beginning of the year I had about ten errors per page. Now I only have three or four. I know that if I use 'Have a Go' and copy more carefully, most of my errors will disappear."

The next few weeks proceed in a similar manner, as I methodically introduce students to word-learning activities they will use throughout the day. Now that we are past the first few weeks, they are ready to try the activities we will use during spelling investigations. I am constantly helping students to look carefully at print and ask themselves, Does this look right?

Materials

- Interesting word (e.g., *affluenza,* a word I found in a newspaper)
- Reading notebook
- *Twilight Comes Twice* by Ralph Fletcher
- *In November* by Cynthia Rylant
- *Nocturne* by Jane Yolen

Categories for Collecting Words

- Interesting words
- Lines that stick in my mind
- Lines that paint a clear image
- Wonder lines
- Words I do not understand but I think are important
- Words I want to understand

Thoughts

A large portion of students pay attention to words only at a surface level. While rereading *What a Writer Needs* by Ralph Fletcher, I became intrigued by the thought, "It seems to me the first shift toward breaking this linguistic stranglehold is for teachers to model our own curiosity with words."

Activity

I like to embed this lesson at the beginning of a read-aloud early in the school year. I tell the students that what I know about myself as a reader is that words grab my attention. This leads into my story about finding the word *affluenza* in a newspaper. Curious students begin to infer what this word means; they break it into parts and connect it to *influenza.* Horror stories of childhood illness fill the classroom for the next few minutes. I put my two cents into the conversation by saying I think the author wanted me to think about a horrible disease.

Then I leaf through my notebook, showing the kids words I have been collecting. I say, "Today, while I am reading, I want you to write interesting words in your notebooks. We will talk about your words during the story and also after the story."

I pick a text with words interesting to me that I want to talk with students about. During the first few read-alouds, when I ask students to collect words, I stop probably more than usual.

Word Savvy: Integrated Vocabulary, Spelling, and Word Study, Grades 3–6 by Max Brand. Copyright © 2004. Stenhouse Publishers.

What's in a Name?

Materials

- Large sheet of butcher paper
- Markers
- 4" x 6" index cards
- Name card model

Thoughts

The first word study lessons focus on the students' first names. Students' first names demonstrate the complex learning of sound, pattern, and meaning that we will explore over the course of the school year. Learning about root words will be fundamental, and names seem to be at the root of who we are. I want this first learning experience to anchor our word study thinking and incorporate good social lessons. As I have planned for the first few weeks of school, I want these activities to help build community. This type of activity not only gets students to begin exploring word concepts but helps them become familiar with each other as they learn to listen and respond to their classmates and me. The first few days' word study activities are designed to teach students the structure of the essential word study activities and that through this structure we will grow as a community of learners.

Activity

I share with students the index card I have designed to let them learn something about myself. I talk them through the thinking process of how I mixed color, symbols, and pictures with the letters in my name to help them learn about me. I tell students that I want to learn more about them and that this activity will help me get to know them.

I pass out the cards and watch the students begin work. There are often many false starts as students notice what classmates are doing and begin to borrow ideas from them. For this reason, it is a good idea to have twice as many index cards as students in your room.

I stroll around the room, planning notebook in hand, noticing and noting: who sits with whom, work habits, procrastinators, leaders, and those who try to copy my model.

As the students are finishing up, we begin to sort the names in a way that makes sense to the students (this year the girls wanted a category for shoppers).

| # Name Origin

Materials

- Chart paper
- Markers
- Word study notebooks
- *The Journey of English* by Donna Brook

Thoughts

I like to get students interested and thinking about the origin of words, labels, and acronyms as soon as possible in the school year. Reading the book *The Journey of English* by Donna Brook helps create an interest in word origins. The first formal homework assignment I assign my class is to interview parents or family members who would know the origin of the student's first name. This is a seed activity that helps me get students interested in word origins.

Activity

I share with my students a story about a good friend of mine named Tylene. Tylene was a miracle baby. She was born in a taxi that had to stop at a gas station on the corner of Tyler Avenue. Her mom put *Tyler* and *gasoline* together, creating *Tylene*. I'm not sure Tylene's mother knew how to spell *gasoline*. It makes for an interesting conversation.

I then ask the students how many of them know where their names came from. Usually, most do not but would like to find out.

I ask, "If we were to interview our parents, what questions would we want to ask them to find out where our names came from?" While we brainstorm questions that would give the students the information they want, I record the questions on chart paper.

The students copy questions they think they will need while interviewing their family members to discover how they were named.

The students return to school the next few days with stories and notes about the origins of their names.

Word Savvy: Integrated Vocabulary, Spelling, and Word Study, Grades 3–6 by Max Brand. Copyright © 2004. Stenhouse Publishers.

Name Sort

Materials

- Large sheet of butcher paper
- Name cards from What's in a Name? (Lesson 3.2)
- Word study notebooks
- Pencils

Thoughts

I envision my students being able to detect and correct their own spelling errors. To help them develop this ability, it is critical from the beginning of the year to demonstrate how to attend to spelling features during word study activities. Allowing students to sort words in various ways helps them pay attention to differences in how words are spelled.

Activity

I gather my class so they can all see the cards from the What's in a Name? lesson. I tell them that yesterday we did an "open sort" of names and that they had determined the categories for sorting the names. Today, I will take certain names and put them at the top of a chart, and these will be the *key words* for today's sort.

I pick names with one, two, and three syllables (see Figure 3.3). I like to sort the students' names by syllables because the most frequently occurring misunderstandings have to do with spelling patterns related to syllables. All the names that I place under the *key words* would have the same spelling feature as the key words.

I start rearranging the students' names under the key words. I like to put two or three names under each key word and then let the students guide me as I place the rest of the names.

Once this part of the activity is done, I ask, "What do you notice?" We discuss their observations as I guide them to thinking about the number of syllables in the names.

Students then record their thinking in their word study notebooks.

Materials

- Chart paper
- Two or three demonstration words
- Word study notebooks
- Pencils
- Students' reading material

Thoughts

We feel challenged to help students transfer what they are learning in word study block to their everyday work. We all know the frustration of teaching lessons when students have trouble staying focused. To combat this, I begin most of my word study explorations with word searches. I ask students to look through their reading materials and class charts to find words that are spelled using the concept that was introduced during the focus lesson. Students learn how to skim and scan for features as they search for and locate words. Rich conversations accompany the search, as students have to monitor whether the word they found truly fits the feature being explored. The students don't complain about lists of words that have no meaning to them. Students have ownership of these lists because they generated them.

Activity

I begin with a quick focus lesson where I present one or two clear examples of the spelling feature or principle the students will explore and use. The students record the exemplars at the top of a clean page in their word study notebooks.

The students locate reading material and skim and scan this material for words that fit the spelling feature or principle. I roam the room, supporting and questioning students as they search, locate, and record words in their word study notebooks.

After about five to seven minutes, we reassemble by the chart stand to record words that the students have found. While I write the words on the chart, the students copy words they did not find in their word study notebooks. I try to spend no more than five minutes writing words on the chart. I collect notebooks and complete the chart later.

I then ask the students to reflect in writing about what they learned during the word search. We create the first few reflections together to ensure that they understand how to write a reflection about their learning.

I do not allow my students to use dictionaries during word searches.

Materials

- Chart paper
- Student writing samples
- Word study notebooks
- Pencils

Example Words

These are words I have used as examples. They came from my students' writing or from my selection of words that would demonstrate a useful spelling feature.

stranger

together

example

appearance

brightness

daffodils

berries

woodland

awful

identical

Thoughts

I like to think of this activity as an introduction to self-assessment of spelling and editing skills. This activity works well during the third or fourth week of school, after I have developed a bond with the students and have their trust as a mentor. Word observations teach the students to systematically look across words and note spelling features. I introduce the phrase "look across the word" during this lesson. This will be a phrase used often during mini-lessons and editing sessions. My goal is to get students to look closely at their spelling.

Activity

I write on a piece of chart paper a word that I noticed the students having difficulty with spelling correctly. I tell the class, "This word is a word many of you have misspelled in your writing. We are going to take a closer look at the word to help you spell words that are difficult for you to spell correctly."

I ask the students to "look across the word" and tell me what they notice about the word. Often I am met by blank faces or unsure expressions. I demonstrate how I look across a word, beginning with the consonants, then moving on to the vowels, then the syllables and other features. When I have finished this demonstration, I ask the students to tell me what they noticed I did.

I record their observations on a chart labeled "Word Observations." This chart becomes a reference for the students as I ask them to do this task independently. We also add to this chart as the students write more complex words that have features that need to be noted, and as they develop competence as word inspectors and spellers.

Word Savvy: Integrated Vocabulary, Spelling, and Word Study, Grades 3–6 by Max Brand. Copyright © 2004. Stenhouse Publishers.

Word Connections

Materials

- Chart paper
- Students' writing
- Demonstration word
- Practice word
- Word study notebooks
- Pencils

Thoughts

Word connections lessons are important because we are demonstrating and discussing with our students how the brain works. Students need to understand that they are using existing knowledge as they work with new or novel information. I have found the term *word connections* confusing to students who may have used it during reading instruction but did not understand the purpose for the connections.

When choosing a word to demonstrate this thinking activity, I try to find one that is part of my students' conversational language, and one that they all can read but most are still struggling to spell correctly. I use the students' writing to choose a word. This helps the students buy into the lesson.

Activity

To begin the lesson, I tell the students we are going to do an activity called Word Connections. I explain how this activity will help them remember words they are having difficulty spelling: "You will learn how to connect the spelling of a challenging word to that of a known word."

I write in the middle of a piece of chart paper the example word for this activity. I show the students where they have been having difficulty spelling this word. I then highlight or underline this part.

Underneath the word I write two or three words that have the same spelling feature. Each time I underline the similar part and tell the students how this connection helps me remember how to spell the exemplar. Students may offer words once I have demonstrated this procedure.

Students are assigned a practice word as they learn how to do this activity.

The group comes back and we discuss how this activity will help as the students read and write. We begin creating an anchor chart titled Word Connections.

Word Savvy: Integrated Vocabulary, Spelling, and Word Study, Grades 3–6 by Max Brand. Copyright © 2004. Stenhouse Publishers.

Word Sketch

Materials

- Inquiry notebooks
- Pencils
- *Ordinary Things* by Ralph Fletcher

Thoughts

Poetry is the music of my classroom. Students read aloud and discuss favorite poems or their own poems. First circle begins with a poem, a line of poetry, or a seed idea for a poem that has been stirring in the students' minds or my mind. Students discover the magical words of many poets as we set aside time each day to reflect on poetry. Poetry helps shape students' thinking as they listen to poems and discuss images, feelings, and thoughts. They grow accustomed to the ritual of listening to a poem being read (usually twice) and being asked what they think. Once this instructional ritual has been established, little prompting is necessary to begin a thoughtful conversation.

Students are asked to consider the phrases and words that help shape their images. Students draw sketches to help them visualize their thinking, and they discuss their thoughts with classmates. Words and phrases are included, as students become cognizant of their own thinking. Discussion may lead them back to the poem as they re-vision their thoughts and understanding.

Activity

I begin the Word Sketch ritual on the first day of school. I enjoy reading the introduction to the "Walking" portion of *Ordinary Things*. This becomes a metaphor for the beginning of the year.

After the second reading, I ask the summer-dazed group, "What do you think?" I break the conversational ice with talk about what images and thoughts this poem brings to my mind.

I then read the poem a third and maybe a fourth time, emphasizing certain parts where Ralph Fletcher has helped me see him beginning his walk. I also ask the students to think where Fletcher has helped them develop an image.

We discuss their images. I may have to prompt them to include the words or phrases that helped them create their images.

The next few days I reread this poem and others from this book. I ask students to draw quick sketches of their images and to write down the words that helped them create these images. We share sketches and thoughts as we reflect on our understanding of the poems.

*Time to leave my desk
and leave the house,
pulling the door behind.*

*I walk the way I write
starting out all creaky,
sort of stumbling along,
looking for a rhythm.*

*Each footstep is like a word
as it meets the blank page
followed by a pause
before the next one:
step, step, word . . .*

Stretch the Sketch

Materials

- Class set of copies of a poem from *The Sidewalk Racer* by Lillian Morrison or *Baseball, Snakes, and Summer Squash* by Donald Graves
- Pencils

Thoughts

I extend the thinking from the Word Sketch lesson and ask the students to sketch on a copy of a poem that has become part of the class archives. The students get an opportunity to personally examine a poem, such as "The Sidewalk Racer," and mark up features that are important to them. Students begin to understand how poets use words, phrases, economy, rhythm, rhyme, and form as crafting tools.

One of my favorite poems to use as introductory poem is "The Bully," in *Baseball, Snakes, and Summer Squash* by Donald Graves. This poem provides opportunities for thoughtful talk about images from selected words and phrases.

Activity

Stretch the Sketch is a morning investigation that students work on when they first arrive at school and prepare for our first circle discussion.

Students sketch images on a copy of the selected poem. They sketch these images as they reread the poem and think about important words and phrases as these relate to their understanding of the poem.

Students bring the finished sketched-on poem to first circle as a tool for class discussion.

Students keep a folder of poems that I select at the beginning of the year. As the year progresses, the class and individual students select poems, which are added to class discussion and the folder.

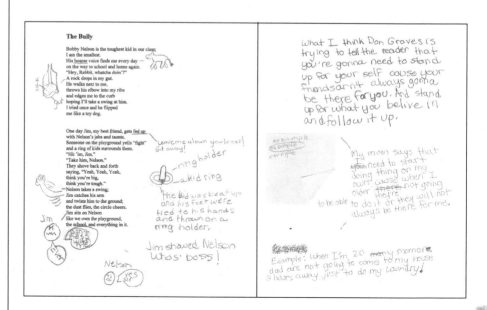

Materials

- Chart paper
- Writing sample on overhead transparency
- Students' first-draft writing
- Post-it notes
- Highlighters

Thoughts

Editing is one of those tough skills we seem to teach over and over to our students, with mixed results. While my students were at the editing stage of their writing, I would get a bit frustrated as they dashed off to grab dictionaries. The dictionary seemed to slow down the momentum of their writing. This slowdown caused two things to happen. First, the most competent spellers did most of the spelling correction. This resulted in a second bigger problem: momentum was lost on the writing itself. As I was trying to come up with an example of how to simplify this process, I thought about how I "have a go" on a scrap piece of paper while writing. I brought this idea to the kids and they said this was similar to what they did in the primary grades. We adopted the title Have a Go because it fit what they were trying to do. This became another strategy the kids used as a tool for looking at words.

My goal is to have students examine their own spelling, learn how to look across the words, and become aware of their own spelling errors.

Activity

I gather my class to examine an overhead of a writing sample. The sample I use has two or three spelling errors. We read through the piece together, looking for spelling errors. I highlight the misspelled words.

On a blank overhead I write the misspelled words, leaving space so that I can write underneath them. I tell the students where the misspelled word does not look correct. I then write a word that I know has the same spelling feature. Next, I rewrite the misspelled word using the spelling feature to see if this looks correct.

Once I feel the word looks correct, I transfer the correct spelling to my writing by drawing a single line through the misspelled word and writing the correct spelling above.

The students take their own first-draft writing (learning logs or content responses) and go through the same process. I usually do this type of lesson on consecutive days. Then I discuss with them where and how they will use the learning from this lesson.

Word Savvy: Integrated Vocabulary, Spelling, and Word Study, Grades 3–6 by Max Brand. Copyright © 2004. Stenhouse Publishers.

Rethinking Spelling

There are many people in adult education courses who have found that spelling can be no barrier to excellent writing. The difference is they have put spelling in its place in the composing process, and have found ways to get help with difficult words, have learned their blind spot on spelling words, and have found some very good editors or friends to help them.

Donald Graves (1994, 188)

The class huddles around the easel, word study notebooks opened to a fresh page. Brad and Nick try to squeeze into the front row, when only a month ago they positioned themselves on the periphery as fence sitters. Many of my students have anticipated the day's lesson, titling their page Have a Go.

The kids amaze me. In six short weeks, the rituals and routines are established and used without prompting. I still focus the group with, "Today we are going to have a go with a couple of words. Will you please title your clean page Have a Go?" Proudly Laura announces, "Did it!" Dan turns to Joseph and says, "I hope they're hard words." I wonder to myself, Are they ready for the challenge of today's lesson?

I write a frequently misspelled word on the chart in front of my class, *belive* (see Figure 4.1). The group reads the word correctly, "believe," as they copy the misspelled word into their word study notebooks. Surprised, Nick tells the group, "That says be-live." "You're right, Nick, it would be read 'be-live.' Now that I have reread my spelling, where is the misspelling?" Before Nick has a chance to answer, a chorus of voices informs me that the spelling mistake is located between the *l* and the *v*. I pull out

Figure 4.1 *Believe* chart.

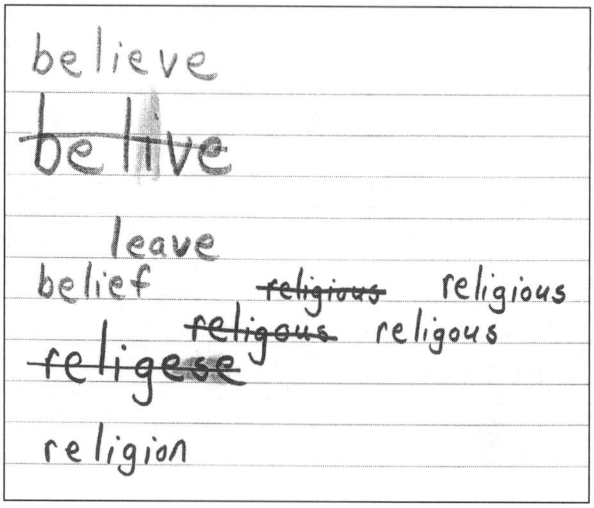

a different-colored marker and highlight my mistake while the group underlines this part of the word.

"I want to correct the spelling of this word. What do I know that could help me?" is my next prompt. Morgan answers, "*Leave* will help." I write *leave* under the misspelled second syllable. Morgan smiles, looking at what I have just written. "*Leave* sounds like the second syllable, but it doesn't look right." "What else could I try?" I ask. Abby answers uncertainly, "*Belief?*" I add *belief* to the chart under *leave*. Later we will go through the same brainstorming process with the word *religious*.

"How will *belief* help me, Abby?" Silence, followed by, "If you know the root word, *belief*, all you have to do is drop the *f* and add *v* and *e*." I cross out *belive*, then write the correct spelling above. This is similar to what I want my students to do when rereading and editing their first-draft writing.

Students need focused spelling instruction like this. Allocating ten or fifteen minutes from my daily language arts time is one of the ways I try to meet my students' orthography needs.

Spelling lessons occur naturally across the day as my students wrestle with spelling features while writing in content area curriculum. Throughout my teaching career, I have viewed spelling as a convention of writing. Spelling has been included in either the writing or language arts section of progress reports. The convention of spelling has social ramifications—it is important in classrooms, where students read peers' writing and publication is part of the writing process. Teaching spelling as a convention has made me reconsider the purpose of spelling instruction and spelling tests.

Spelling Development

Rethinking the purpose of spelling tests has taken me away from the idea that a list of memorized words will help me assess my students' developing knowledge of English orthography. Reading students' writing in tandem with spelling research has helped me understand the developmental stages of spelling.

The spelling assessments that I administer to my students are composed of words that help us monitor their orthographic knowledge. These assessments are composed of words that I notice have challenged my students' spelling knowledge, words that are frequently misspelled in first-draft writing, and unknown words. The purpose of the last is for me to see what strategies my students apply to unknown words.

I do not require my students to memorize any lists of words. The results of the assessments will help us understand their spelling needs as we set spelling goals.

Letter Name
- Words spelled using dominant consonant sounds or letter names (e.g., KT for *cat*, Y for *why*, MAK for *make*)
- Words spelled using short vowels (students learn many single-syllable high-frequency words)

Within Word
- Words spelled using long vowels (e.g., CVCe)
- Single-syllable words spelled using common long-vowel patterns (e.g., r<u>ai</u>n, l<u>ea</u>f, f<u>igh</u>t, b<u>oa</u>t)
- Single-syllable words spelled using *r*-controlled vowel patterns (e.g., p<u>ar</u>k, d<u>ear</u>, sp<u>or</u>t)
- Single-syllable words spelled using consonant patterns (e.g., <u>qu</u>it, <u>spr</u>ing, <u>thr</u>ow, ki<u>ck</u>, bea<u>ch</u>)

Syllable Juncture
- Words spelled dropping *e* and adding suffixes *-ed* and *-ing* (e.g., *baked, taking*)
- Words spelled that have a doubled consonant, or that need consonant doubling, at the syllable juncture (e.g., *battle, planning*)
- Words spelled using syllable stress influence on vowels (e.g., *remain, ready, ceiling*)
- Words spelled with prefixes and suffixes (e.g., *en-, for-, in-, re-, -ion,-ment, -ly*)
- Compound words, homophones, and hyphenated words

Derivational Constancy
- Words spelled with silent and sounded consonants (e.g., *autumn, doubt, muscle*)
- Words spelled with pronunciation changes (e.g., *music/musician, recess/recession*)
- Words spelled with Latin-derived suffixes (e.g., *comfort<u>able</u>, incred<u>ible</u>, not<u>able</u>*)

Figure 4.2 Developmental spelling features (adapted from Ganske 2000).

Kathy Ganske's (2000) and Edmund Henderson's (1990) stages of spelling development have helped me identify spelling features that my students are wrestling to control. I have adapted terminology and descriptors from their research to use while planning for spelling instruction (see Figure 4.2).

Figure 4.2 is an overview of the stages of spelling development. I always use caution when classifying students based on developmental features—students may exhibit characteristics of more than one developmental stage. I use the stages to help me think about students' spelling confusions. Which spelling features are challenging them while they are writing? I use this information to infer what stage of development the students are at relative to their spelling knowledge.

I want to know whether a student is relying on letter sound strategies similar to a Letter Name/Within Word speller (see Figure 4.2). Students in this stage might have spelling confusions of *litol/little, turtol/turtle,* or *finil/final.* These spellings demonstrate a reliance on letter sounds to represent vowel sounds. This is still a challenging concept for some intermediate-grade students.

Next, I ask myself, Has the student transitioned from letter sound strategies toward using visual strategies to learn and spell unknown words? This is a Within Word/Syllable Juncture speller. I see this type of spelling when Brad works out when to use a silent *e* at the end of words. Nick demonstrates this as well while attempting to spell *during/dering* or *sure/sher.*

Many intermediate-grade students have transitioned to visual strategies, yet they are still working out when to double consonants when adding suffixes to words like *stopping*, or *tugged,* or *bigger.* These students also have difficulty with high-frequency words like *probably* and *different.*

Many intermediate-grade students use both visual patterns and word meanings to learn and spell unknown words, as would a Syllable Juncture/Derivational Constancy speller. Understanding these stages affects the types of activities and words I choose as periodic checkpoints to measure student spelling growth and development. My goal is to find the range of spelling development of the students in my class and then to incorporate formal and informal instruction while supporting the class, small groups, and individuals in their understanding of English orthography.

To help my students develop spelling knowledge, I have devised word study activities that help them learn to notice and remember spelling features. Students participate in spelling investigations in which they learn how to figure out whether a word looks right when they write it during their daily drafting. My objective is to help them transition from relying on letter sound spelling to using visual patterns and word origins as spelling strategies. To help them make this transition, I want them to ask, "Does that word look like it is spelled correctly?" while reading their own and peers' writing as well as published texts. Dictionary skills and using spell-check while word processing both require this skill.

Think of the child who misspells *during/dering,* a misspelling I have seen more than once over the years from students who had *r*-controlled vowel confusion. My computer spell-check has the following four spelling options: *daring, during, dewing,* and *derange.* While the student sorts through the four options, the last two will probably not be considered. Chances are the student's eyes go to the second choice because she has seen the word often. Now, consider the amount of time the same child might spend using the dictionary to look up this word. Students not only need to develop an eye for what "doesn't look right" but also have strategies that help them spell confused words correctly.

Spelling Tests

Do I give spelling assessments? Yes. I give my students pop quizzes about once every grading period (nine weeks). These assessments are made up

Table 4.1 First Spelling Assessment (Given in October)

were	High-frequency word
great	High-frequency word
until	Frequently used and misspelled
different	Frequently used and misspelled
during	Frequently used and misspelled
purpose	Frequently used and misspelled
probably	Frequently used and misspelled
countries	Plural, drop *y* and add *ies*
believes	Plural, frequently misspelled word
themselves	Plural, change spelling of root word
guesses	Plural added to word ending with doubled *s*
tomatoes	Plural added to word ending with *o*
swimmer	Consonant doubling with *r*-controlled vowel in unstressed syllable
beggar	Consonant doubling with *r*-controlled vowel in unstressed syllable
affair	Doubled consonant with *r*-controlled vowel in stressed syllable
fiddle	Unstressed vowel pattern (*le*)
usually	Consonant doubling to add *-ly*
curtain	Unstressed vowel pattern (*ain*)
bargain	Unstressed vowel pattern (*ain*)
using	Drop *e* and add *-ing*
caring	Drop *e* and add *-ing*
ignore	*r*-controlled vowel in stressed syllable
beware	*r*-controlled vowel in stressed syllable
orbit	Content high-frequency word
axis	Content high-frequency word

of twenty to thirty words, depending on the time of the year and the spelling features the class has been studying.

These assessments are unannounced. I want to know what students have been learning through our spelling investigations, daily writing, and editing.

You may be wondering whether I could announce these tests, provide lists, and promote home involvement. Families and students would then fall into past patterns of preparing for the spelling tests by memorizing the words, which is not what I want. In the past when I used traditional spelling tests, students did not always retain the information and apply it to their writing. I want to avoid this pitfall if possible.

One way to involve the family is to ask students to collect words that fit a spelling feature we are studying from home reading materials. Then I include these words on the class list. Students strive to find the most words that fit a spelling feature, and the high achievers search for unusual words.

Third Grade	Fourth Grade	Fifth Grade	Sixth Grade
Plurals (*s, es*)	Plurals (*s, es, ies, ves*)	Consonant doubling	Consonant doubling
Suffixes (*-ion, -ment, -ly*)	Consonant doubling	Homophones	Word families starting with root word
Compound words	Common homophones	Prefixes (*ex-, im-, ir-, in-, un-*)	Prefixes (*pre-, pro-, sub-, inter-*)
Drop *y* and add *ies*	Prefixes (*un-, for-, mis-*)	Suffixes (*-less, -ment, -tion, -sion*)	Suffixes (*-ology, -ation*)
Single-syllable words with long vowels (CVVC)	Suffixes (*-ed, -ing, -ly*)	Contractions	

Table 4.2 Guidelines for Choosing Spelling Words

I use example words, high-frequency words, and content words when putting together a pop quiz. The high-frequency words represent words that students use often and misspell. I may select content words that have been used frequently and that I think students should know how to spell.

To find words that illustrate spelling features, I've used *The Spelling Teacher's Book of Lists* (2004) by Jo Phenix, *Words Their Way* (2003) by Bear et al., and *Word Journeys* (2000) by Kathy Ganske. These resources are invaluable because they have outstanding lists classified by spelling features. I scan the lists and choose words that will challenge my students' spelling knowledge and that will be exemplars for a lesson if misspelled.

I administer the first assessment (see Table 4.1) during the seventh week of school because I want the students to have had an opportunity to develop spelling habits—the habits of learning how to look at words they think may be misspelled, finding their spelling errors, and correcting these errors.

The students have spent time learning my basic six spelling activities—Word Observation, Word Connections, Word Webs, Have a Go, Word Sorts, and Word Searches. They have edited two or three pieces of published writing to consider their own spelling errors and test out the spelling strategies I've presented in lessons. So when Brad tells me, "Slow down, Mr. Brand. I'm having a go," during the assessment administration, I know my instruction is beginning to affect how he thinks about his spelling.

I give the assessment like any traditional spelling test. I say the word, use the word in a sentence, and then repeat the word. Depending on the grade level I am teaching, the spelling list will include frequently misspelled words along with a few spelling feature words.

I try to use the guidelines in Table 4.2 to help me choose words for each grade level. Remember, these are my guidelines. Chances are your state and district have benchmarks that can help guide your list choice.

For more examples of spelling lists I've used at different grade levels, see the Appendix.

These assessments become a tool students use for spelling self-assessment when writing spelling goals. One way I use them to help the students know themselves as spellers is making the following suggestions after they've attempted to spell all the words:

"Circle a word that you have never heard before." (I want to know what spelling strategies students apply to unknown words.)

"Highlight a part of the word that does not look right." (I want to know if students are learning how to monitor their own spelling mistakes, and if they are learning where they typically make spelling errors or where a word may be difficult to spell.)

"Cross out your misspelled words and try it again." (I want to know if students can self-correct their spelling errors.)

"Look at your spelling mistakes. What do you notice about them?" (I want to know if students notice patterns in their spelling errors. If they have trouble consistently with the same spelling features, this might become a spelling goal.)

"What do you think you need to do to improve your spelling?" (I want to know if students can look at spelling errors and begin to think of strategies to help themselves improve.)

You may wonder why I go to this effort when students could use their writing drafts to highlight and correct spelling errors. I have found that it is difficult for students to find spelling error patterns by looking solely at their own writing, especially at the beginning of the year. The periodic assessments have enough words that represent spelling features so that students can notice their own spelling error patterns.

Spelling Goals

When students sit down to write their spelling goals, they use writing drafts, spelling assessments, and my feedback to guide their thinking. The language I ask them to use while writing their spelling goals is specific. It is important that I help them learn how to talk about words and spelling features. I use spelling terminology as a tool to help students notice aspects of words and label them.

1. untit until
2. contry — countries
3. bewere
4. rpose or purpose
5. probibly — Probably
6. swimmer
7. wher — were
8. afaire — affair
9. Tomatzes — tomatos
10. caring
11. grate — great
12. certin — curtian
13. fiddil — fiddle
14. gesses — guesses
15. themselfs — themselves
16. begger — beggar
17. using
18. ignore
19. bargen — bargain
20. ushaly — usual
21. belivs — believs
22. during
23. different
24. orbite — orbix
25. axise — 2x1s

1. untill until
2. countries
3. because
4. Purpose Purpose
5. probably
6. swimmer
7. were
8. afaire affair
9. tomatoes tomatoes
10. caring
11. great
12. curtian curtian
13. fiddle
14. guesses guesses
15. themselves
16. beggar beggar
17. using
18. ignore
19. bargain I thought you said something else
20. usually
21. believes
22. during
23. different
24. orbit
25. axis I thought you said something else

I think I messed up because I don't really know when to have double consonants or just one letter. I also have trouble with vowels and unaccented like beggar you would think that it is er because it sounds like er not ar. I'm bad with vowels because well, what I just said. Sometimes a and e sound alike and it is hard to tell which letter to use. I hope to improve. I usually mess up in the second syllable but it can be in the first syllable.

Highlighted first spelling assessments.

I have found over the years that students like to sound grown up; using spelling vocabulary helps them do that. At the same time, I am helping students focus on important aspects of spelling that they may have overlooked, not considered, or not been ready to internalize in previous years.

When students sit down to write their spelling goals, they have spent six weeks learning and understanding terms like *consonant clusters, vowel patterns, prefix, suffix,* and r-*controlled vowels,* and the concept of syllables. They are still growing in word knowledge and in the vocabulary used to describe features of words.

As we meet to draft spelling goals, it is important for me to create an anchor chart (see Figure 4.3) with questions that prompt students to think about word features, their own spelling difficulties, and how they can improve as spellers. I want my students to consider these items while rereading their drafts—when Brandon is haphazardly using an *e* at the end of words, or when Abby uses *er* while writing most multisyllable words that have an *r*-controlled vowel in the unaccented syllable. Brandon demonstrates this when he writes his simple but specific spelling

Figure 4.3 Anchor chart for editing spelling errors and to help focus thinking on spelling goals.

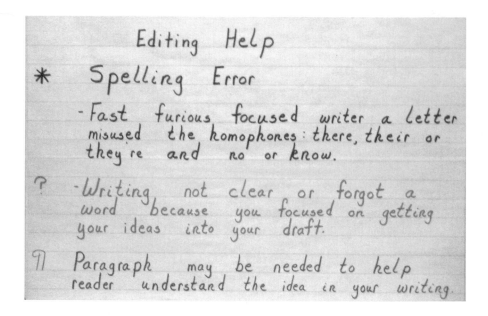

goal: "to remember when and where not to add an *e* on a word." Brandon is right; he needs to focus on his use of *e* as a marker. He is transitioning to using visual information while writing.

Abby has crafted her goal using a more sophisticated spelling vocabulary and knowledge of herself as a learner: "to use Have a Go when I write words like *beggar* because I think *er* but it is *ar*. And *until* because I thought it was *untill*. So I don't know when to double the consonants, and I have trouble with vowels and unaccented words. I would wish to spell things better. And to become a better writer/speller."

I give my students time to develop not only the correct vocabulary but the spelling concepts to help them become responsible learners. The word observation activity helps build this language, and it helps students monitor whether a word looks like it is spelled correctly.

Each time I help my students edit their spelling errors I try to correct their errors using the formal vocabulary. Now when Brandon goes to read a draft, I ask him, "What will you be looking for while you are reading this draft?" His response reflects his goals: "I want to make sure it makes sense, and I want to look at the words that have *e* at the end of them. I'm going to try using a ruler like you showed us to help me focus. Focus is one of my problems." Brandon and I trust each other now, so he can be honest in our conversations.

I have learned over the years that many intermediate-grade students still grapple with a few key spelling features. Vowel patterns in words like *believe, curtain, beggar, affair,* and *usually,* or dropping the *e* prior to adding a suffix, or doubled consonants and consonant doubling in words like *different, usually,* and *actually* are commonly confused aspects of intermediate-grade spelling. While reading my students' writing during the first few weeks of school, I notice and record in my notebook (see Figure 4.4) their confusions and misconceptions about vowel patterns, consonant doubling, and other spelling features so that I can focus their attention on these.

I use Have a Go to clarify some confusions. "Today we will use Have a Go to help us locate some of our spelling confusions. While looking through your writing last night I noticed many of you had some difficulty with a couple of words," I announce to the class.

I write *diferent* on a chart. Melissa asks, "Should we copy this down?" Michael playfully answers for me, "Of course." The students copy this word into their notebooks. I notice Nick, Brad, Jackie, and a handful of other students realizing that this is one of their errors. "This word doesn't look right," Jackie calls out. "What doesn't look right?" I ask. "It needs two *f*'s. I forget this every time I write *different*," Nick tells me.

I could have chosen to leave out one of the *e*'s, another feature students have been neglecting. But during a lesson, I try to focus on only one spelling feature. Usually there are spelling errors that are representa-

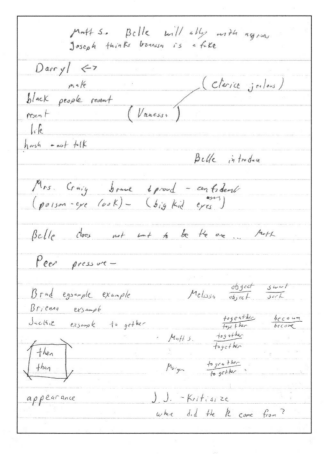

Figure 4.4 My notebook page recording students' spelling confusions.

tive of a Within Word speller (see Figure 4.2) learning about long-vowel patterns. I write misspelled words on a chart. The errors are already underlined to save time and to keep the focus on the confusing spelling feature. Then I tell the students what I notice about my errors. I create an anchor chart to focus my students' thinking as they search their last two drafts and a past spelling test.

Misspelling Anchor Chart
- Count the number of words in both your drafts. Next count how many words you misspelled. Record both these numbers at the top of the page. Calculate your percentage of correctly spelled words.
- Look at your spelling errors. Are your confusions with vowels, consonants, or both?
- If you have consonant confusions, think whether they are about consonant clusters or doubling.
- If you have vowel confusions, think about whether they are with long or short vowels. If you can, think about which syllable the error occurred in.
- If you need help, make a circle so Mr. Brand can help you.

This activity is a good day's work, often bleeding over into writing workshop. I need to take as much time as needed to ensure that students understand what is expected. I like to do a quick go-around-the-circle when I am finished, to help me monitor what the students say they learned about themselves as spellers. "I keep adding an *h* to *were*," Nick thinks out loud. Abby says, "I keep leaving out the *e* in the third syllable of *different*. I never noticed before." "Those words that have vowels with *r* are tough for me," says Drake. "I need to slow down while writing them." I'm pleased when I hear a lot of my "word vocabulary" being used by these nine-to-eleven-year-old kids.

The major goal for much of this work is for each student to write an initial spelling goal. The following day I reassemble the students in front of the misspelling anchor chart and my spelling error chart. I write a goal on a piece of chart paper that uses the spelling error pattern. The written goal becomes a model for students to use when writing their own spelling goals. The students' spelling goals and my notes about their misspellings help me launch the year's first spelling investigation.

Spelling Investigations

I use students' spelling error patterns and spelling goals to plan for the first spelling investigation. During a spelling investigation, I guide stu-

"To be careful on words that have complicated vowels and consonants. I need to be better on the second syllable. . . . I can use the charts on the wall and the dictionary . . . if I don't know a word."

"To remember when and where not to add an *e* on a word."

"One of my spelling goals is when . . . I double a letter when I add a suffix."

"Saying the syllable to spell it right. And also doing Have a Go, and go through the whole word before going to the next, and putting prefixes and suffixes."

"To improve writing suffixes such as *ar* and *er*. To not get mixed up with suffix such as *beggar*."

"To be better at where vowels belong in a word. . . . I will succeed in what my goal is to be a slower and better word speller and vowels. I am a fast writer but still I should think about the vowels before I write."

"I would like to try to accomplish over the next few weeks on words that double the consonant. Also I need to work on dropping the *e* and adding *-ing*."

"My spelling goal for the next few weeks is for me to sound out the words better and to tell *u* from *o* in words in the first syllable. I have a lot of trouble finding my errors because I think I spell them right but I don't. . . . I think Mr. Brand can help me by putting words on walls."

"To use more vocabulary when needed. Like in science and social studies. I will read over my papers to check for vocabulary and add vocabulary when needed. If I don't know how to spell a vocabulary word, I will use Have a Go, then write the word down on a sticky note until I memorize the word."

Students' spelling goals.

dents to look closely at a spelling feature. A spelling investigation typically lasts three to four weeks. During a spelling investigation I help students learn to look at their spelling and know when to use a spelling feature. While taking a close look at a spelling feature, I want to support students toward achieving their spelling goals and help them develop general spelling knowledge.

Since students typically have a variety of needs, I carefully plan what activities, example words, and support my students will need to be able to use the spelling feature automatically while writing. Choosing one or two example words each day helps focus the students' attention on the spelling feature. I interchangeably use the following activities during a spelling investigation:

- Word Observations (see Lesson 3.6)
- Word Search (see Lessons 3.5 and 4.1)
- Word Connections (see Lesson 3.7)
- Have a Go (see Lesson 3.10)
- Helping a Friend (see Lesson 4.2)
- Take a Good Look (see Lesson 4.3)

- Web the Word (see Lesson 4.4)
- Word Sort (see Lessons 4.5 and 4.6)

I like to begin the spelling investigation with the word observations activity. When choosing a feature word, I try to find a word that students are misspelling in their writing. I use a word that displays the spelling feature and that students are familiar with. I used the word *beggar* from my first spelling test because a majority of my students misspelled this word and I was investigating the spelling feature of unstressed syllable vowel patterns.

I write the word on a piece of chart paper and ask students to write it in their word study notebooks and then write all they notice about this word. While the students are writing their observations, I watch and confer with them. I may pull a small group to the side and prompt them to notice and record spelling features. After a few minutes, I pull the students together and record their observations on the chart. I then talk with them about the focus spelling feature, ensuring that the group begins to focus on this characteristic of the word.

The students take the time to work on penmanship while copying *beggar* into their word study notebooks. "Hey, that's one of the words I spelled wrong on my spelling test," Matt comments. "Me, too," Jackie laughs. Most of the group confesses that *beggar* was a challenge. "What do you notice about *beggar*?" I prompt. "It has two syllables," a few students call out. "You double the *g*'s," Melissa reports. Abby says the *ar* is difficult. "I thought it would end with *er*—that's how it sounds." "Sometimes the way a word sounds is not enough to help you spell the word," I tell the group. "We are going to start investigating the different ways *r* influences the spelling of vowels." "This will help me," Nick mutters under his breath. Tomorrow I will use *summer* for my word observation so that the students can begin to create lists with me to help sort out their *r*-controlled vowel confusions.

During the first semester I like to have the students do the word observations activity during the first two days of a spelling investigation. Then I ask them to go on a word search, looking for words in their reading material that has this spelling feature. Students search for words for approximately five to seven minutes and record them in their word study notebooks. I chart the students' discoveries, leaving a column for words that do not have the spelling feature. Table 4.3 outlines a three-week spelling investigation of *r*-controlled vowels, focusing on *er, ir,* and *ur.* During this investigation, we created a chart showing words with *er, ir,* and *ur* vowel patterns.

I help students focus on the spelling feature by being very explicit with my prompts and questions. Since spelling investigations typically last three weeks, students anticipate my prompting. This anticipation helps them notice features in their own work because they know that I

Day	Activity	Lesson Focus
1	Word Observations	*purpose*
2	Word Observations	*burglar*
3	Word Search	Chart students' discoveries
4	Word Connections	*surgeon*
5	Word Sort	Use list from Day 3
6	Helping a Friend	*curious, purchase*
7	Word Observations	*circus, person*
8	Word Search	Chart students' discoveries
9	Word Connections	*virtue, prefer*
10	Take a Good Look	*surface, thirsty*
11	Take a Good Look	*serpent, confirm*
12	Have a Go	Writing sample with *er, ir, ur;* spelling errors
13	Helping a Friend	*version, twirler*
14	Web the Word	*firmly, burrito*
15	Word Sort	Use lists from Days 3 and 8

typically find examples in their writing or use words that will stretch their understanding of a spelling feature.

"Today we are going to underline the *r*-controlled vowel," I inform the group as I write *curtain* on the chart. Joseph laughs as he copies *curtain* into his word study notebook. "Got me! I keep writing *certain* for *curtain*. I know, *r* vowels in first syllable. Killer. I tell myself to slow down." Katie adds, "Oh—*murmur* is like *curtain*. I misspelled it in my story." The students begin to understand the examples and the lessons, and where these will meet their spelling and writing needs. It is teaching students to focus their eyes on challenging and confusing spelling aspects.

I focused on this spelling pattern because my students had been using incorrect *r*-controlled vowel patterns. They had not had enough experience using visual knowledge when the sound of letter combinations was similar. The students discovered that most of the example words used during the lessons had the vowel pattern in the first syllable. The word searches prompted students to create another chart with multisyllable words with *er, ir,* and *ur*. The investigation also included dialogue about stressed syllables, suffixes, and consonant doubling. Even though my focus was on this particular vowel pattern, my students became more conscious of vowels in general, especially those controlled by *r*. I show them how this spelling feature is similar to the one in words they know, like *dollar* and *cellar*.

Investigations similar to this one help my students learn to look at and talk about spelling. I want my students to become aware of the way words look. I have found that with many of the spelling features there are single-syllable as well as polysyllabic words. Since a range of words can be found that fits the spelling pattern, most investigations meet the needs of the entire group.

During the year there may be times that my best spellers do not participate in an investigation or activity because they have already mastered the spelling feature being discussed. When this occurs, these students use this time to work on writing projects.

High-Frequency Words

High-frequency words constitute another area of spelling that I try to incorporate into spelling investigations and student writing. My goal for high-frequency words is that they be written quickly and spelled automatically. I know that words such as *certain, different, possible, special,* and *thought* have spelling features that challenge students' memories. Since they present a challenge, I want students to have experience with high-frequency words that will allow them to monitor and self-correct misspellings.

During a spelling investigation I often slip in a high-frequency word that students are misspelling and focus on the part of the word that is confusing them. Helping a Friend and Take a Good Look are activities that support automatic spelling of high-frequency words.

On a cabinet that my students can see while writing, I post frequently misspelled words (see Figure 4.5). I change these monthly. I want my students to internalize the spelling of these frequently used words and eventually not to need this visual aid. Students who have difficulty remembering these words also include them in a personal word bank at the back of their word study notebooks as a reference. Students suggest words that they think should be posted on the cabinet.

These words are usually introduced one or two at a time weekly. I use about five minutes during our Tuesday morning meeting to introduce them. I try to keep the following guidelines in mind when introducing and monitoring students' mastery of high-frequency words:

- Display one or two words students frequently use and misspell.
- Highlight the part of the word students have difficulty spelling.
- Use the word in a sentence (humor helps) so students understand the meaning of the word.
- Refer to the word during shared writing and writing conferences to support students who need extra help.

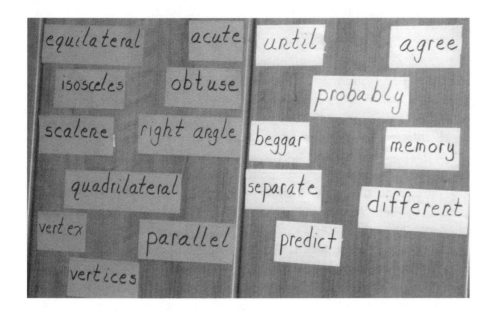

Figure 4.5 High-frequency words posted on a cabinet next to math words.

- Monitor students' use of these words in their writing so that they will come to spell them correctly automatically.

Posted words are a temporary support toward correct spelling. My goal is for students to learn these words so that they can spell them automatically while writing. Words I notice a large portion of my class misspelling that are used frequently in daily writing are posted. When posting a word I demonstrate ways to remember it by looking at spelling features.

For example, *predict* is a word my students frequently use during reading workshop and have a tendency to misspell. Most students' spelling confusion was with the first syllable. Jackie and Nick mispronounced this word, and their reliance on a sound spelling strategy resulted in *predict* being spelled *perdict*. Matt, Chris, Abby, and a few others visually confused the *r* and *e*. While posting the word, I cleared up this confusion: "While reading your reading logs I noticed many of you had some trouble spelling *predict*. *Predict* is the kind of word I take a moment and think about how to spell it when I write it. What I found helps me is to think about what the word means. To me it means to tell before I read what I think will happen. I know that the prefix *pre-* means 'before,' as in the word *preheat*. You know, to heat an oven before cooking."

I write *predict* on a piece of tagboard, demonstrating with a hyphen between the syllables, *pre-dict*. I invite students to copy the word in their word study notebooks as I did, *pre-dict*.

"I want you to think about the prefix *pre-* when you write this word or when you're rereading your writing," I say. "If you need to look on the cabinet for the next few days, that is fine, but I would like this to be a word that you can write quickly, since we use it almost every day." If possible, I try to introduce frequently misspelled words before students use them in their writing. I know that concept words in math, science, or social studies will be challenging. I know my students will ask me how to spell them because they value spelling words correctly in their writing. I try to anticipate my students' questions.

I do not want lessons to bog down, but I appreciate and respect my students' desire to learn how to use and spell a sophisticated group of words. For this reason I try to introduce any words quickly, in a way that will help the students remember how to spell them and not develop an overreliance on the posted words. I encourage students to place these words in their word banks at the back of their word study notebooks. I leave a word posted for as long as I feel the students' developing fluency and automaticity is being supported. I may post one or two words a week. Many students record these words in their word banks in their word study notebooks.

Spelling and Writing Drafts

I have learned that posting words on a wall or cabinet is not enough for helping students use and spell words correctly. I view writing as thinking. To support my students' thinking about spelling features, they note, collect, generate, and reflect daily about words in their word study notebooks. The spelling activities I use are participatory, so that students develop knowledge of English orthography. I ask students to date and record the titles of spelling activities. The title of the activity signals to the students the type of thinking and learning that will be expected from them during instruction. I use chart paper to demonstrate how to format a page for an activity and explain the purpose and intention of the activity. Students begin to adjust the way they format their pages for activities as they think about how an activity will support their learning. I have found that using reproduced pages has not resulted in the depth of thinking and knowledge that I sought.

I also ask students to attach a word bank inside the back cover of the word study notebook. This word bank is a personal collection of high-frequency words that the student uses and misspells. I want to help students learn correct spellings and use them in their daily writing. In some cases, not enough students misspell a particular word for it to be included in a list of posted words, and thus it can take its place in individual word banks.

I have also observed that there may be a variety of reasons that students spell words incorrectly in early drafts of writing. At the beginning of the year, I mark an X in the margin next to lines of drafts from writ-

A agree accute always	B	C	D disagree different*	E equlator equilateral each
F	G	H isosocles	I	J
K	L	M memory	N	O obtuse
P probably parallel	Q quadrilateral	R	S scalene	T they
U until	V vertices vertex very	W	X/Y	Z

Student's word bank at the end of October.

ing workshop that have spelling errors. I do this because often students by fifth grade have been misspelling a word for a long time and need help spotting their spelling errors.

Next, I ask students where they think this word is misspelled. If they can tell me and know the correct spelling, I ask them to put a line through the misspelled word and correct it on the draft. If they are unaware of where the word is misspelled, I show them. I then ask them to try it again on a sticky note. If they still do not spell the word correctly, I write the correct spelling on the sticky note. Then I ask them to include it in their personal word bank. These words are arranged in alphabetical order.

My goal is detection and correction of misspelled high-frequency words. When students write words in their word banks, I note this in my planning notebook. My goal is for students to demonstrate that they have learned to spell the word correctly in their daily writing. On occasion, students may take their notebooks home and study their own lists. Students do need to learn to remember how to spell words correctly, particularly words they are frequently misspelling in their daily writing.

I do not grade the word study notebooks. The way I evaluate the effectiveness of this tool is by monitoring my students' spelling in their daily writing. I look to see how they are applying concepts that they are learning and note the number of spelling errors in relation to the number of words written. The students' writing provides me with information and words I will use as I plan for the next spelling investigation.

Students still need to find the misspelled word and correct it. I record students' misspellings in my planning notebook to help me discover the patterns and stages of students' spelling development.

I want students to be thinking about spelling features during spelling activities. I like to bring closure to spelling activities by asking students to reflect on what they have learned. At the beginning of the year, I model this thinking by using the just completed chart of the activity to show students what I wanted them to learn. I may use a highlighter to help them see connections. Once students are comfortable with this type of thinking, I use the following prompts to ask students to reflect in their word study notebooks:

"Take a minute and think about what you just learned about [a word]." (This holds students accountable for their learning. If I get standard, redundant answers, this prompt may need to be changed, or I need to push the child to think a bit more about the activity.)

"Tell me what it is about [a word] that you have learned." (This focuses students to be more specific about their learning, and it becomes the focus for instruction.)

"Take a minute and think about how what you learned about [a word] will help you." (This helps students think about their spelling goals. It also helps them envision how the thinking will help them while writing. My students often comment on the editing process, thinking about rereading to detect and correct spelling errors prior to publication.)

This may sound like a lot of work, but it is not when I consider the alternative. I remember using weekly spelling lists. I remember cringing each time I corrected the spelling tests. I remember students who did not study and kept on missing many words. I remember smart students who memorized only the weekly feature but not the entire word. I remember how students played the "spelling game."

Some kids just have trouble spelling words. But with all the tools available, they can learn to recognize their strengths and weaknesses while working toward final drafts that have minimal spelling errors.

I want students to be responsible for a majority of the spelling work. I try to help them learn about words and how they work so that they can detect and correct their own misspellings.

Reading Text Word Search

Materials

- Students' independent reading texts
- Word study notebooks
- Rulers (optional)
- Chart paper
- Pencils

Spelling Features to Use for Word Searches

- Long-vowel patterns
- *R*-controlled vowels
- Dropping letters to add suffix
- Consonant doubling
- Plurals
- Possessives
- Prefixes
- Suffixes
- Latin root words
- Greek root words

Thoughts

I like to have students search for and gather words during an investigation of a spelling feature. They like scouring through their reading materials to find examples of the spelling feature we are investigating. I have found that while students are searching for feature words, many opportunities arise to teach them how to connect sound spelling features with visual spelling features. Once students finish collecting words and recording them in their word study notebooks, these words are recorded on a chart, then used for word sorts the next day.

Over the years I have learned that students need a demonstration on how to scan a page of print with a ruler as they try to locate spelling feature words. This is a valuable lesson that is useful across the curriculum as students look back for information in content studies.

Activity

I like to begin this activity by reviewing what the spelling feature looks like. Words used during word observations are good review words. I write a word on a piece of chart paper and ask students to write it in their word study notebooks. Then I take the book that I am reading aloud to the students and tell them, "Today I am going to scan my reading book for words that have the same spelling feature as ——. I am looking for words that have the —— feature."

I then show students how I use a ruler to scan down the page and move across a line of print. While scanning, I tell them what I am looking for. Once I find a word, I write it on the chart and visually check the word by looking at the spelling feature.

The students search for spelling feature words from their independent reading materials. I ask them to find between four and eight words. I do not want this to be a time-consuming process. Students seem to add to their own lists during independent reading.

The next day I record the class's words on a chart. Once again, this is a wonderful time to clarify students' understanding of the spelling feature. You can collect word study notebooks and record the words on the chart at another time.

Word Savvy: Integrated Vocabulary, Spelling, and Word Study, Grades 3–6 by Max Brand. Copyright © 2004. Stenhouse Publishers.

Helping a Friend

Materials

- Overhead transparency or chart paper
- Frequently misspelled word
- Word study notebooks
- Pencils

Frequently Misspelled Words

difficult

develop

favorite

finally

generous

height

instrument

organize

probably

purpose

separate

until

Thoughts

The idea for this lesson came from work I had been doing with my students in math. In my classroom we do a lot of cooperative learning activities in which students become peer coaches. Students needed help learning how to help their classmates without providing the correct answer or response. Students often read and edit each other's work. Instead of relying on the class spelling gurus or myself, I knew guidance was needed to enable them to be independent. The premise of this lesson is to show the class the misspelled word on chart paper or an overhead and have the students find the error, then offer words that will help spell the misspelled word correctly. I would suggest some word connections lessons prior to this lesson.

Activity

The lesson begins with students looking at the chart paper or overhead projection that has the misspelled word displayed. For example, I might choose the word *captain*.

I begin by saying, "My friend has misspelled this word. Do you see where the confusion is?" The students direct me to the misspelling, and I underline this portion of the word. Then I prompt them to take a minute and in their word study notebooks write some words that can help my friend with the spelling mistake.

I circulate, noticing the students' thinking. This is a good time to confer or prompt a student who has a hard time generating connections.

I draw the students' attention back to the misspelled word and play-act working with my friend. I record suggested help on the chart paper or overhead transparency and make explicit how this will help. Explicit language such as "the miscue is in the second syllable" or "if you know how to spell *captain,* it will help you with the second syllable in *Britain*" is used so that students can find the misspelling independently.

Word Savvy: Integrated Vocabulary, Spelling, and Word Study, Grades 3–6 by Max Brand. Copyright © 2004. Stenhouse Publishers.

| # Take a Good Look

Materials

- Overhead transparency or chart paper
- Commonly misspelled word
- Word study notebooks
- Pencils

Commonly Misspelled Words

enforce
enforse
inforse
inforce

instrument
instrement
instrament
instriment

colonies
colonys
coloneys
colones

separate
seporat
seperate
separat

Thoughts

I love reading students' writing. They have nice voice and are developing skills for writing in a variety of genres. As often as I coach myself not to look at the spelling miscues, they still jump out at me. I decided to start writing the different misspellings of frequently used words in my planning notebook. Then I devised a lesson to help students look across the words more carefully. The students like this lesson because they know that I am paying attention to their errors and giving them a strategy to fix their errors while writing. We assume students know how to monitor their spelling, but often they do not rely on visual strategies. This lesson is easy and quick, and one I do every two to three weeks.

Activity

This lesson begins with the students looking at a list of three or four ways to misspell a frequently written word. I also include the correct spelling in the list.

I prompt the students by asking them to "look carefully at the list of words and write the correctly spelled word in your word study notebook. Underline that part of the word that is difficult for you to remember while writing this word."

I circulate, noticing the students' thinking. This is a good time to confer with a student who is having difficulty looking across a word and distinguishing where she is making spelling errors.

Once the students have done this, I underline the correct word. We then brainstorm words that have the same spelling feature and talk about how knowing and remembering the spelling of these words can help while writing the targeted word or with checking their spelling.

Once students are comfortable with these procedures, they write the correct spelling and the list independently. I usually emphasize two words during a Take a Good Look session.

Web the Word

Materials

- Overhead transparency or chart paper
- Preselected word
- Word study notebooks
- Pencils

Thoughts

I like to help children explore the spelling feature that I am focusing on in depth. Once students have had exposure to spelling features, we consolidate this knowledge by webbing out a word. Knowing how to look carefully at words in isolation is critical to helping students search and scan in the sea of print they are writing or reading. I like to have examples in my students' heads that stick out, so that when they have a question while writing or reading, they have an exemplar to guide their thinking. Exploring a word in depth that stands out as an exemplar is critical in helping children develop the ability to monitor, detect, and self-correct their errors.

I have found these lessons very helpful when exploring the spelling concept of doubling a consonant when adding a suffix. I also use them to teach students about consonant or vowel alterations when there are pronunciation and spelling changes.

Activity

The students gather around the easel or the overhead screen. I have already written the example word on it. I like to use *shop* or *plan* as I introduce this activity for consonant doubling. *Expand* or *invade* work well in demonstrating the idea of a consonant alteration (*expansion, invasion*) with a spelling and pronunciation change.

I ask the students to copy this word into their word study notebooks. I tell them, "We are going to make a word web that will focus on suffixes, so there needs to be enough space to do this. We are going to start at the top and first add the plural ending *s* to the word."

The lesson continues with me saying the word with the *s* added prior to writing the word. I tell the students I visualize what the word looks like and then write it down. I check my spelling to see if it looks right.

The students copy what I am writing as I do it. I ask, "Does it look right?" If it does not, we stop and have a conversation about why the spelling looks strange.

I then add a second word and let the students go through the same process themselves.

Word Savvy: Integrated Vocabulary, Spelling, and Word Study, Grades 3–6 by Max Brand. Copyright © 2004. Stenhouse Publishers.

Word Sort

Materials

- Chart with list of words
- Word study notebooks
- Pencils

Spelling Features to Use for Word Sorts

- Long-vowel patterns
- *R*-controlled vowels
- Dropping letters to add a suffix
- Consonant doubling
- Plurals
- Possessives
- Prefixes
- Suffixes
- Latin root words
- Greek root words

Thoughts

I have discovered that many student spelling errors are a result of using the sound-it-out strategy to spell words. Even some of my better spellers still rely on sound when they attempt to spell words that they do not have a visual image for. I know that students are often befuddled when I ask them if a spelling looks right. Word sorts have allowed me to help students sort out vowel patterns that sound the same but can be spelled more than one way. I then add to these lists as students find words that were not used during initial sorts.

I like to use the back of the word study notebook for word sorts. I like the students to have ready access to these lists and ask them to add to them during the school year.

Activity

The lesson begins with students looking at chart paper with a list of words found during our reading text word search (see Lesson 4.1).

I begin by saying, "Today we are going to sort the words we found during our word search into groups." (I try to have only twelve to fifteen words on the first lists and then increase based on the spelling feature under investigation.) I then scan the list and find three words as exemplars to sort words into spelling feature categories.

I write these words at the top of a piece of chart paper. The students copy my model. Then I demonstrate how to scan the list, categorize a word by spelling feature, and then write it under the exemplars. The students copy my model. During the first demonstration I usually work through half the list. The students finish the sort by themselves. When the students finish, I record the remaining words to be sorted on the chart.

I ask the students to write what they learned during the word sort. I prompt them to think how this will help them while writing.

W	P	I
Where	Passed	their
~~Weighed~~	paced	toes
Wade	paste	there
Ware	past	
~~does~~	g	Other
~~allowed~~	goes	does
~~aloud~~	guest	allowed
	~~guessed~~	aloud
		mist
		missed
		board
		here

Materials

- List of words to sort
- Chart with list of words
- Word study notebooks
- Pencils

Thoughts

Word sorts are a great activity to help students pay attention to patterns in words. Word sorts help students categorize and group like words together. I've adapted common approaches to sorting in an effort to help students become independent. I also do not want to spend an inordinate amount of time preparing materials or use a lot of instructional time.

I have used this activity in place of a spelling test with great success. Students are required to listen to words and record them in their word study notebooks in spelling feature categories. Students correct their work and self-correct their errors during a ten-to-fifteen-minute word study block.

Activity

I preselect between nine and sixteen words that fit the spelling feature the class has been exploring. I also record the key words at the top of a piece of chart paper or an overhead transparency. A key word should be a word that was used to demonstrate the feature and is well known by the students.

I ask the students to turn to a clean sheet of paper in their word study notebooks, date it, and title it Word Sort. Then I write on a chart the key words and ask the students to copy them and make columns so they can write words under these words.

I dictate my word list, using each word in a sentence. The students write the word in their word study notebooks in the column under the key word.

Then I gather the students around the chart or overhead and write the dictated words under each key word.

I discuss confusions as the students correct their work and self-correct their errors. The error discussion focuses first on categorization and use of spelling features, then on errors in spelling and what students notice about the pattern of their errors.

Word Savvy: Integrated Vocabulary, Spelling, and Word Study, Grades 3–6 by Max Brand. Copyright © 2004. Stenhouse Publishers.

Pretesting Word Knowledge

Materials

- Overhead transparency or chart paper displaying spelling words
- Preselected spelling words for test
- Word study notebooks
- Pencils

Sample Word List for Test

This is a list I used. The list comprises words my students were constantly misspelling in their writing as well as words with silent consonants.

character

soften

assign

arrest

protest

doubt

balance

opposite

direction

until

altogether

probably

Thoughts

If I want my students to learn how to monitor and self-correct their spelling errors, then I need to teach them how. A spelling test is something you feel responsible to give your students—fine. Parents like spelling tests. Helping children memorize lists of words is one way parents feel they can support their child at home. If you are going to give your students a list of words to learn, you may want to assess them at the beginning of the study to see what they already know about these words and their own spelling strengths. I suggest using the pretest as a learning tool.

Activity

I read my students' writing to see which concepts they are having difficulty understanding and which fit patterns of misspellings. I like to have a list with between twelve and fifteen words. I choose easy, mildly challenging, and challenging words and arrange them on the list in a mixed-up order usually beginning with the first two words to be less challenging.

I administer the pretest, using each word in a sentence. The children record the pretest in their word study notebooks.

Next, I ask students to circle any word they have never heard before. Then I ask them to put an X in the left-hand margin next to words they think are misspelled. Once they have identified words they believe may be incorrect, I ask the students to underline where they think they misspelled the word.

I display the correct spelling on a chart or overhead. The children correct their errors, noting where their errors occur in a word. Then they write a one- or two-sentence reflection about what they learned about themselves as spellers.

Word Savvy: Integrated Vocabulary, Spelling, and Word Study, Grades 3–6 by Max Brand. Copyright © 2004. Stenhouse Publishers.

To Capitalize or Not?

Materials

- Overhead transparency or chart paper
- Word study notebooks
- Pencils
- Fiction or nonfiction text used for an investigation

Common Capitalization Miscues

battle/Battle of Lexington and Concord

king/King George III

war/War of 1812

congress/The Congress

revolution/The American Revolution

Thoughts

While my students are crafting notes, outlines, observations, or reports, they wonder about which words to capitalize. I realize that my state's standard has listed this as a second-grade objective, but many students are puzzled by the idea of proper nouns. In social studies they run up against confounding words like *battle, war,* and *king.* When and why are these words sometimes capitalized and other times not? To support and guide my students' understanding, I have designated a section of their word study notebooks for proper nouns they may use in their writing. These words are noted in the notebooks and posted on charts. The searching, recording, dialogue about, and use of these proper nouns has helped my students develop an eye for capitalizing while writing.

Activity

My students have their word study notebooks divided into sections. I begin the conversation with, "I noticed in your writing the last few days many of you forgot to capitalize some important words. These important words are called proper nouns. A proper noun is a name, a name of a place, battle, war, or title that is given to someone important."

At this point I write on my chart a proper noun, *King George III.* "I capitalized *king* because it is part of King George's name and title. While you are reading from your social studies book today, I want you to record proper nouns in your word study notebook. When we are all finished reading, we'll record what we found on the chart."

I allow students time to read and record proper nouns in their word study notebooks. Then I record students' discoveries. I like to have a copy of the text the students read so that if there is confusion, I can reread and talk through the difficulties.

My students have found this to be a handy section of the notebook because they often keep track of important ideas and concepts that relate to the essential inquiry question.

Word Savvy: Integrated Vocabulary, Spelling, and Word Study, Grades 3–6 by Max Brand. Copyright © 2004. Stenhouse Publishers.

Developing Vocabulary

Sometimes I've spent weeks looking for precisely the right word. It's like having a tiny marble in your pocket; you can feel it. Sometimes you find a word and say, "No, I don't think this is precisely it." Then you discard it, and take another and another until you get it right. What I'd like to stress above everything else is the joy and sounds of language.

Eve Merriam (1990, 66)

It's early November, Saturday morning; I'm driving my two oldest sons to skating lessons. The window is cracked. The radio is turned up an extra notch, forcing my five-year-old son Joel to "shout sing" about bare-naked trees that line our drive. I'm lecturing my son Max about the scientific reason behind leaves falling from trees.

Suddenly, he brings my scholarly thoughts to a halt—not to question me about my talk, but to ask about the tune on the radio. Max is caught by the rhythm of Peter Gabriel's *Lovetown* as it reverberates through our vehicle. Max begins to sing the catchy chorus to himself: "I'm living in lovetown." Then in an inquiring nine-year-old voice he asks, "What does *lovetown* mean?" An interesting question—at first I'm not sure how to answer. I reply using my teacherly tone, "What does *love* mean?" I'm prompting Max to break the word into parts, in the same way that I do at school with my students. Max responds enthusiastically about love, relating the feelings he has for his mother.

I press on, trying to get him to connect *love* with *town:* "Now, think about what *town* means."

"I know, a place where people live," he explains. A bit confused, he searches for clarification by saying, "I still don't get what *lovetown* means. Why would you put those two words together?" The song has no useful context to help Max sort out his thinking. His limited background knowledge of the subject of this song makes it impossible for him to make sense of the word *lovetown*. I know that any explanation I offer will only prompt further questions into subjects I'm not ready to investigate. Since it is Saturday morning, and I realize the concept of this song is over his head, I cop out by saying, "You're too young."

Children create and wonder about language as they encounter it in a variety of forms. Joel invented a phrase, "bare-naked trees," to describe the leafless trees he saw. I hear invented, colorful language from kids at the ball field and skate park. I have trouble making heads or tails of this invented language at times, until the participants explain the words and their meaning. These explanations often include why the word was coined. This terminology is a cultural phenomenon that participants use to describe actions, stunts, plays, or other parts of the activity.

Insider vocabulary is used as a rite of membership into any activity or club. The words and phrases are known by the kids because of their participation in these activities. Children carry this language learning knowledge into the classroom; the trick is getting them to become owners of the school vocabulary. This will allow them to demonstrate knowledge of content and learning.

Vocabulary instruction is a tricky business. Teaching students skills and strategies for building vocabulary and using their developing vocabulary is an ongoing process. Not knowing what students understand about concepts and content confounds the problem of building vocabulary. My instruction for vocabulary is built on the following premises:

- I need to build new concept understanding while developing vocabulary.
- I need to help students relate background knowledge to new concepts and vocabulary.
- I need to show students how to use context to infer the meaning of words.
- I need to show students how to use word parts to infer the meaning of words.
- I need to provide multiple opportunities for my students to use new vocabulary.

The key is establishing an inquiring classroom in which students have opportunities to explore their thinking through conversation, reading, and writing to promote vocabulary development.

Conditions That Support Vocabulary Development

Word detectives are hidden in our classrooms, waiting for the opportunity to show their ability to uncover knowledge of words. "Teachers should be more interested in promoting new words as a way to enable students to conceive and express new ideas. The primary goal of vocabulary instruction, therefore, at least after the initial stages of reading, is not to teach students new labels, but to teach them new concepts" (Nagy 1988, 21).

Vocabulary instruction is a way to develop students' speaking, reading, and writing lexicons. The goal is not just to have students build a richer vocabulary but to develop strategies for this development. "Good

Literacy vocabulary links.

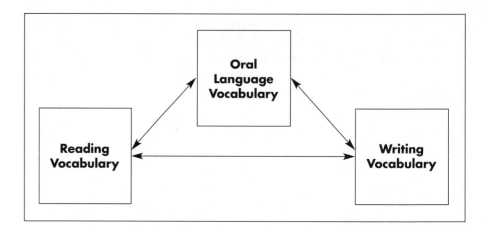

language users select the appropriate meanings of words from a large number of possibilities. Even the simplest words often have more than one meaning and many shades of gradations of meaning" (Leu and Kinzer 2002, 324). My instruction has to help students understand the power of words, how to craft words while speaking and writing, and how to understand words encountered during daily reading.

Conversations before, during, and after reading experiences as well as shared writing and writing conferences are opportunities I use to support and extend vocabulary. I want students to have the chance to discuss and use their developing vocabulary knowledge in supported

Students use their inquiry notebooks to infer, play with, and use content-rich language.

settings prior to independence. There are teachable moments for learning new vocabulary daily. Some are planned, and many others come about because our students are curious word learners.

Some conditions that support vocabulary development are the following:

- Teachers are fascinated by language and share their interest with their students.
- The classroom is alive with playful and thoughtful interactions with language.
- Language is a tool for thought as students and teacher share, explore, and refine their thinking about curriculum content.
- There are multiple opportunities to inquire, wonder, and delight in learning experiences.
- There are multiple opportunities to think about words while reading, writing, and learning content material.
- The classroom walls are draped with print that is meaningful to the learners and organized by the learners.
- The classroom is an experience-oriented one, where language and vocabulary develop as students build and refine their understanding of "big ideas" or concepts.

Thinking Through Vocabulary Plans

To help my students expand their reading vocabulary I plan a variety of reading opportunities from multiple genres daily. Nagy (1988) suggests that the "single most important thing a teacher can do to promote vocabulary growth is to increase students' volume of reading" (38). Just increasing students' independent reading will not be enough to expand their vocabulary without support and strategies for understanding words. A balanced literacy program that flexibly uses read-aloud, shared reading, and small-group strategy instruction along with independent reading where vocabulary is explicitly taught and discussed supports vocabulary development.

My mind constantly puzzles over the idea of how many words children may not understand while yet comprehending the text they are reading. I've adopted some specific questions I use to probe students' vocabulary knowledge. While conferring with a student, I often overuse my favorite probing questions: Did you understand that word? Did you notice ——? What do you think —— means? Why do you think the author used that word?

Pretty soon students are anticipating my questions or asking themselves these same questions whether I am there or not. To get students independently asking themselves this type of question takes time, patience, understanding, continual demonstrating, coaching, and prompting while applauding partially correct responses.

Where do I begin? How quickly do I move? and When will I see results? are the questions I continually ask myself as I try to move students to this level of independence in learning new words.

Where Should I Begin?

Timing is important. Not wasting time is even more important. One of the more challenging vocabulary skills that I work to sort out with my students is recognizing interesting important words. I want my students to think about word choice and how this affects them as readers. I later bring this thinking into writing workshop as I guide students to use this skill in their own writing.

It is one of the first days of autumn, and the kids are catching on to the daily ritual of reading aloud after lunch. While the students are opening their reading notebooks and positioning themselves around the circle, I read the title of the chapter "The Wayward Gull" from Cynthia Rylant's (1995) *The Van Gogh Café*. I read it twice, as I do with poetry, letting the magic of Rylant's writing dance in the students' minds.

Chris asks, "Did I hear right? You said the 'weird word gull'?" Michael gives Chris an odd look. I repeat *wayward* for a third time as I move toward the easel to write the confusing word on a piece of chart paper. "The Wayward Gull," I read again. This time the students see the word *wayward* as I read it aloud. I ask, "What do you think *wayward* means?" Silence, as the students look to each other, hoping someone answers, anticipating something more to come.

I continue. "I think *wayward* is an important word. Cynthia Rylant must have had a purpose for using *wayward* at this point in the book." "Yeah, she wants us to stop and get us to think," remarks Michael. "What do you think she wants us to think about?" I challenge him. "I'm not sure, but *wayward* is weird." I ask the group this time to think with me and use our background knowledge to infer what *wayward* could mean.

"This story has been about magic, ordinary magic," Laura informs the group. Trina asks Laura, "Do you think it is only magic? There has to be something more. How does this all connect with Van Gogh?" "Yeah," says Joseph. "I keep on thinking about ordinary things, stopping to look, noticing like in that Fletcher book and Van Gogh's paintings." Joseph points to Fletcher's *Ordinary Things: Poems from a Walk in Early Spring*. Sydney steers the conversation to thinking about how Van Gogh may

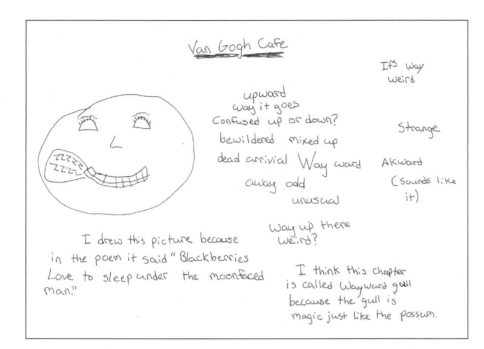

have lost direction in his artwork. He kept moving, searching. "He seemed very lost."

I ask the kids to think about the setting of the story. Josh answers, "Kansas. The bird is lost." I refocus the group to help me think about the meaning of *wayward.* "Let's web the word now and then read the story and see if we can understand Cynthia Rylant's use of *wayward.*" While creating a word web (see Lesson 4.4), students think about how strange the word is. I ask them to break it into syllables and think through how *way* goes with *ward,* using *forward* to infer direction.

We spend time organizing our thinking to help us infer what *wayward* could mean. We use background information from the story and word parts. We think where the story could be headed and how it could be parallel to Van Gogh's life, then we read on, looking for clues in the wording and story that will help us understand *wayward.* "Mixed up," "confused," and "odd" are noted during the reading and recorded in most students' notebooks. Morgan adds "bewildered" into the mix, a word we had thought through earlier in the year and the students are now comfortable using.

My goal is to get students to think more carefully about the author's choice of words. How do these words get the reader/listener to stop and think? Why did the author choose to use this word to express this thought? Once I have pushed the students to think about words in this way, I need to help them develop strategies for thinking about the meaning of these words, often unfamiliar words.

Model for independent word learning.

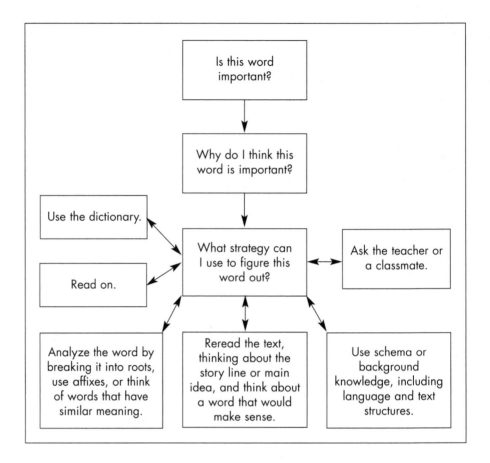

I now teach vocabulary in the context of actual reading because of student comments during reading conferences. When I would ask a student the meaning of a word that I thought he might not understand (but that was important to the story), I was likely to hear one of the following responses: "I know what it means, but I can't say what it means" or "I can't explain what it means, but you know it means . . ." or (my favorite) "I can't put my tongue on it." I agree it sometimes is difficult to "put your tongue on" your thoughts. My goal is to show students a variety of ways to use background knowledge and the text to infer meaning and understanding of unfamiliar words, or familiar words used in unfamiliar ways.

Questions I want the class to think about while I am reading aloud or they are reading independently are Was this word choice intentional? What are the author's words trying to get me to think about? Why this word?

My questions become the basis of an anchor chart (recorded thoughts and reminders on chart paper) that we create to help focus our thinking about vocabulary. The anchor chart is posted within eyesight of our meeting area so that the questions can easily be referred to before reading aloud or as a prompt for thinking during silent reading. I also create another anchor chart that supports the students' thinking about how they could infer the meaning of unfamiliar words.

I focus on developing vocabulary skills and strategies throughout the year by asking these questions: Do my students monitor (know) when they do not know the meaning of a word or phrase? Do students know which unfamiliar words or phrases are important so they understand the main idea of the text? Do students have any strategies for inferring word meaning? Do students infer word meanings?

How Quickly Should I Move?

I have found that short texts work well in supporting students' marking of vocabulary. I try to pick a text that will be interesting and help them develop an eye and ear for marking up texts. At the beginning of the school year a majority of my class was absorbed in reading the Unfortunate Events series by Lemony Snicket. In *Time for Kids—Exploring Nonfiction* there was a book review of the eighth book, *The Hostile Hospital.* I prompted students to read the article, thinking about words the author used to describe the eighth book.

I wanted the students to learn to mark a text for a purpose and also to note words that they could begin to use while writing their own book reviews. We created an anchor chart of review words (see Figure 5.1). The

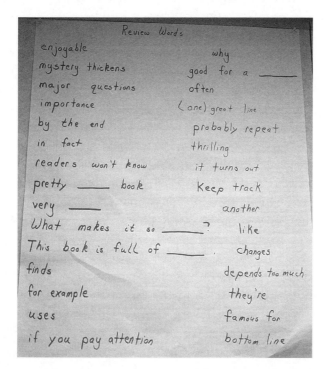

Figure 5.1 Anchor chart of book review words.

students also kept a section in their word study notebooks that they added to over the course of the next week and the remainder of the school year.

Students read other book reviews over the course of the next week. After reading each article, we added words to the list, noting how book reviewers use similar words while writing book reviews. Once students understand how and why to highlight words, I have them read articles to monitor, locate, and infer the meaning of unfamiliar words.

Once I feel that students are locating what is important, I move on to talking about monitoring unknown vocabulary. I want students to recognize when they do not understand a text, and to locate words that they did not recognize or understand. I use a previously read text, often one from the first week, which students keep in a folder. I use a familiar text while introducing new thinking so that the students can apply their thinking toward the new skill or strategy. My conference notes, along with student notebook entries, comments, conversations, and assignments, help me judge how quickly I move in my instruction and expectations for independent application.

We settle into the afternoon ritual of stretching our thinking (see Lessons 3.8 and 3.9) during read-aloud. I am reading my students *Hoot* by Carl Hiaasen because this book is the type of novel that often is overlooked or abandoned by most of my students. *Hoot* is a great read because it addresses environmental concerns, standing up for what one believes, loyalty, and other issues that affect the world of my students. The complex story structure would be a challenge if read independently by many of my fifth graders.

While reading and previewing *Hoot,* I realized this book would provide ample opportunities for the students to dig deeply into the author's point of view and have thoughtful conversations. The author, Carl Hiaasen, uses interesting vocabulary that would provide fuel for both planned and spontaneous vocabulary learning.

The children gather in a circle around my rocking chair, preparing their reading notebooks for our focused read-aloud. We complain about another inside recess ("Will winter ever let up?"). Then I begin reading, "Roy zipped through his homework in an hour," which is the first sentence of Chapter 5. Abby politely interrupts to remind me that students who were out of class yesterday need to know what they missed.

There is a brief recap of how the main character, Roy Eberhardt, stood up to two bullies. The conversation also extends to the vandalism at Mother Paula's Pancake House construction site. Most of the students feel they know who the vandal is and suggest I begin reading.

I make it to the end of the second paragraph when I hear a collective "Huh?" I reread the last sentence: "Twenty minutes later, he arrived at

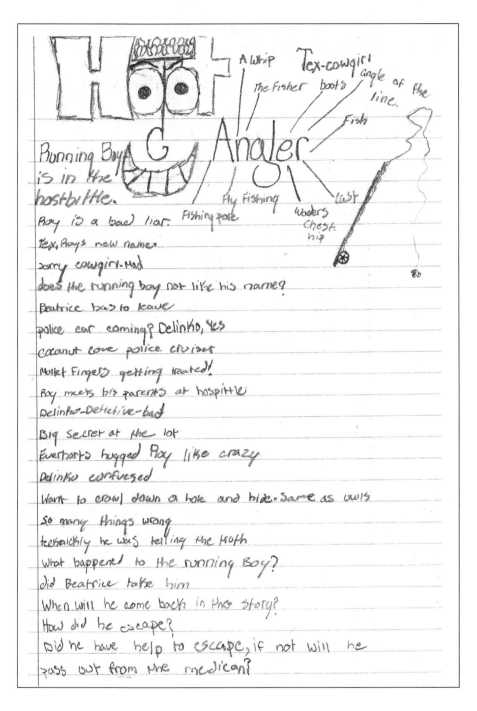

Student's reading notebook entry on *Hoot*.

Beatrice Leep's bus stop, and from there he easily retraced Friday's ill-fated foot chase." Kelsey breaks the silence with, "I don't get it."

"Get what?" I respond.

"Ill-fated," Kelsey moans.

Drake now joins the conversation by asking, "Could you read the sentence again?"

Brienna pushes me one step further and suggests that maybe we should read the next sentence or two and see if that will help. "Yes!" I think to myself. How many times have I mentioned this important strategy? Brienna heard me. Maybe now some of the others will remember it, too.

I read the next paragraph, and most of the students are still confused. I circle back to the paragraph that began this teachable moment. Prior to rereading, I ask the students to write the word *ill-fated* in their reading notebooks: "This sounds like a word that may be important in helping us understand what is going on in the story." Brienna asks for the spelling of *ill-fated*. I pull out the dry-erase board and ask Jackie how you would spell *ill*. She volunteers *i, l, l. Fated* is a bit more difficult; a handful of students ask me to write the word *fait*, spelled like *faith*. I put both suggested spellings (*illfated, illfaited*) on the board and prompt the group to tell me which spelling looks right. Dan, my resident spelling champ, has been holding back. He says the first word would look right with a hyphen.

The class copies *ill-fated* into their notebooks. Prior to rereading, I ask the class what is going on in the story. I also ask them to think about what had happened to Roy in the story on Friday. Chris says, "Roy was chasing the running boy across the golf course and got whacked by a golf ball."

Now as we think about *ill-fated,* we also need to think about the word *retraced.* Joseph tentatively answers that he thinks the word means "bad luck." "It comes from ill—being sick. That made me think of 'bad,' and 'fate' is like a bad outcome. Roy got struck by a golf ball and had to see the vice principal, so it was bad luck." Tyler jumps in and says it is like A Series of Unfortunate Events, where the children are always running into Count Olaf.

Once I finish the chapter, the students begin to think about their silent reading. I challenge them to use background knowledge and to think about how words are put together while they try to infer word meaning while reading.

The students are reading silently, and I make my way across the room, looking at reading logs and checking in with Abby because she was not sure what she was going to read. Abby tells me she wants to think about *Nocturne* by Jane Yolen because she thinks she may have missed something when I read it aloud. Sydney is next up on my conference list.

Sydney is reading MacLachlan's *Sarah, Plain and Tall.* She directs my attention to her reading log and inquires about the meaning of the word *mild-mannered.* "Remember what we talked about during read-aloud with *ill-fated*?" I prompt. "How could you use the same strategy to help yourself?" She responds, "*Mild* is like cheese; it is either hot or mild." I encourage her to go on. Sydney thinks a bit more and says, "*Mannered* comes from *manner*. Like how you act. Your mannerisms. Mild mannerisms. I think she's low-key like me."

Mild-mannered makes its way into our classroom conversations as we discuss a class representative to meet with the district food service supervisor about changes that the fifth grade think will improve food service. A meaningful context with guided support helped Sydney relate background knowledge as she inferred the meaning of an unknown word. Then Sydney had the chance to use this word in what she felt was an appropriate situation. The class liked this term and added it to our class word wall (see Chapter 7).

When Will I See Results?

Vocabulary instruction is a constant challenge as I support students in their growing knowledge of words and word meanings. I have to remind myself that vocabulary instruction is not an all-or-nothing science.

When Sydney stops and asks the meaning of *mild-mannered,* I am seeing results. When my students take the time to record and figure out the meaning of unknown words in their reading logs using background or context clues, I am seeing results. When my students take the time to use words they have highlighted and recorded while reading book reviews in their own book review writing, I am seeing results. When Tyler rushes through the door with his writing notebook in hand to show me how he has used *meandering* in his writing, I am seeing results.

I take the time to praise these vocabulary moments and highlight them for the whole class. Then Brad wants to share how he borrowed Sydney and Michael's thinking. The praise leads to more students' independently giving a strategy a try. If I want to see results, then I need to provide daily opportunities for my students to read, write, and think about both word meanings and word selection while writing.

Katie's reading log for Janeczko's *A Poke in the I* (see Figure 5.2) is a good example. She comes across the word *smitten.* She first questions whether this is a word or not. Then she poses a question to herself about the meaning of the word. Katie uses the picture and the placement of the words in her attempt to infer the meaning.

Katie is exploring words she may be a little young to understand, but she is influenced by café life. This word *smitten* is hard to grasp but was great for showing students how to use a root word like *smite* and the ideas in the poem to infer meaning.

Figure 5.2 Student's reading log entry on *A Poke in the I*.

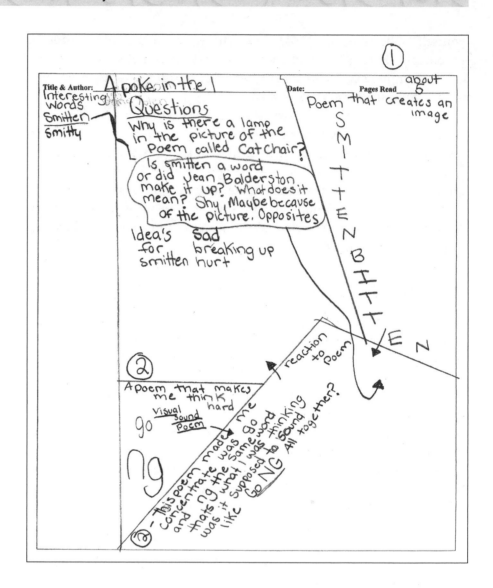

I need to ensure that the classroom promotes inquiry about the meaning and use of new words as students learn how to use these words during conversation, writing, projects, and drama. Chapter 6 focuses on the challenge of supporting vocabulary development in specific content area contexts.

Using Context While Reading a Book

Materials

- Overhead transparency or chart paper
- *Pedro's Journal* by Pam Conrad or *The Witch of Blackbird Pond* by Elizabeth George Speare

Excerpt from *Pedro's Journal* by Pam Conrad

"Everyone was smiling and so friendly. Close up, we could see how clear and gentle their eyes were, how broad and unusual their foreheads. The captain especially noted and said to one of his men, 'See the gold in that one's nose? See how docile they are? They will be easy. We will take six back with us to Spain.'" (39)

Thoughts

Our students read historical fiction, science fiction, realistic fiction, and novels that stretch their thinking. The vocabulary students encounter while reading these genres is challenging. The challenge often is that the concept the language depicts or illustrates is new to the reader. In the balanced literate life of my students' day I encourage them to read nonfiction daily. My goal is to help students use the context of the text they are reading along with background knowledge to understand new concepts. This lesson is similar to Use the Clues to Infer Meaning (see Lesson 6.2).

Activity

I like to teach this lesson while I am reading aloud historical fiction. The steps are simple, but the power lies in the demonstration of your thinking and getting your students to think along with you.

I write an excerpt from the text on a chart or overhead transparency. I choose *docile* to demonstrate my thinking because it is an interesting word choice by the author and represents how Columbus perceived the natives.

I read the selection aloud to my students. When I read the word *docile,* I comment to my students, "I think this word is very interesting. I wonder what Pam Conrad wanted me to think about here." I finish reading the remainder of the journal entry (four short sentences).

Then I think aloud, "*They will be easy.* What will be easy?" I continue by explaining that I think Columbus thinks that the natives will be easy to capture. He wants to take some natives back to Spain to show off to the king and queen. I then remind the students about our background knowledge of Columbus and explorers. Columbus thought he was smarter and better than anyone else. I think this is important in helping me understand why the author used *docile* to describe the natives.

I think *docile* has something to do with being easily persuaded and trained. This is similar to what the Portuguese did to the Africans they enslaved.

I then discuss the thinking I did with the students. I demonstrate my thinking during the remainder of the text. I create a chart that describes the thinking I want my students to do.

Word Savvy: Integrated Vocabulary, Spelling, and Word Study, Grades 3–6 by Max Brand. Copyright © 2004. Stenhouse Publishers.

How Do I Pronounce That Word?

Materials

- Overhead transparency or chart paper
- Overhead copy of character pronunciations
- *Who Built the Pyramid?* by Meredith Hooper
- Word study notebooks
- Pencils

Names in the Pronunciation Guide for *Who Built the Pyramid?*

Senwosret

Montuhotep

Imhotep

Nakht

Senebu

Amenemhat

Ameny

Inyotef

Thoughts

Most students leave third grade with a fluent knowledge of phonics. Even though students understand phonics, the daily content reading material often has words that students have never heard or seen. Textbooks and nonfiction reading materials often have pronunciation guides that support students as they read independently. I have found it useful to help students learn how to read and become successful using these embedded supports. Meredith Hooper's book *Who Built the Pyramid?* has a wonderful pronunciation guide that can be used as a primer to demonstrate syllable breaks. This pronunciation guide highlights stressed syllables, which is a very slippery concept for many students. Students also enjoy this story, and it can be read aloud or used with a small group.

Activity

For this lesson I combine "how to" with inquiry. I need to briefly explain what a pronunciation guide is and how it helps the reader pronounce words, and then assess how well my students identify syllable breaks.

"Today we are going to read *Who Built the Pyramid?* by Meredith Hooper," I say. "This book has character names that are hard to pronounce. Meredith Hooper has included a pronunciation guide to help the reader read the names. While using a pronunciation guide, it is important to know how to see and read syllable breaks."

I write the first word from the pronunciation guide on a chart or overhead, *Senwosret*. I look at the word, then divide it into syllables (Sen-wos-ret). "While I looked at the word, I thought about syllables and our talk about vowels and consonants in each syllable," I explain. "Next, I mentally broke the word at these points and looked at the pronunciation guide [I show the group the overhead of the pronunciation guide] so that I could read the word."

I write the next word (Montuhotep) on the chart or overhead and ask the students to write the word in their word study notebooks and break it into syllables. We then view the overhead of the pronunciation guide. I point out the accented syllable.

We move through the entire guide this way and then enjoy the story. During the story we refer to the guide and discuss how it helps during the reading.

Word Savvy: Integrated Vocabulary, Spelling, and Word Study, Grades 3–6 by Max Brand. Copyright © 2004. Stenhouse Publishers.

Discovery Note Taking

Materials

- Chart paper
- Inquiry notebooks
- Pencils
- Nonfiction reading materials

Useful Nonfiction Texts

Time for Kids—Exploring Nonfiction

Write Time for Kids

Textbooks—short sections

Time for Kids, featured article

National Geographic for Kids, featured article

Thoughts

It seems like sometime in each school day I am preaching about the importance of organization. I want my students to organize their workbenches so they can take advantage of learning opportunities. I have found that note taking is an organizational tool my students enjoy exploring and using. Note taking makes my students feel mature as they begin to organize their discoveries while reading, watching a video, or listening to a guest speaker.

I know that the inquiry curriculum in which I try to engage my students depends on organization, discoveries, asking questions, and recording key vocabulary. With this in mind, I ask my students to read nonfiction reading materials using their inquiry notebooks and dividing their pages into three section headings: Discoveries, Questions, and Key Words. Students have found that their discoveries while reading have led to questions for further investigation. The key words section has helped students note and record important words and new vocabulary. These words often find a spot on a class list of important words. My goal, of course, is to help students use this vocabulary in content conversations and in writing.

Activity

I like to start note taking once students are comfortable highlighting important information from a text. I typically use a *Time for Kids* passage to help students learn to take notes.

The students independently read a preselected text. Once all the students have read the text, we assemble in front of a piece of chart paper that is divided into three sections: Discoveries, Questions, and Key Words. The students bring their copies of the text and inquiry notebooks (students learn how to manipulate these tools).

I reread the text, stopping to record my discoveries on the chart. I tell the students why this is a discovery and usually have a question or two that this discovery makes me think about. I record the questions, leaving space for answers.

Often my discoveries have key vocabulary words included in them. I also write this important vocabulary in the section titled Key Words. I explain that as I review my notes, this key vocabulary often helps me remember important ideas. I also want to use this vocabulary when I write about this topic.

Word Savvy: Integrated Vocabulary, Spelling, and Word Study, Grades 3–6 by Max Brand. Copyright © 2004. Stenhouse Publishers.

| # Collecting Important Words

Materials

- Overhead transparency or chart paper
- Yolen and Stemple's *Roanoke: The Lost Colony, The Mary Celeste,* or *The Wolf Girls*
- Inquiry notebooks
- Pencils

Important Words Anchor Chart

A word is important because

- It says the big idea.
- It is an unfamiliar word.
- We have to think about the meaning of the word.
- It is a new vocabulary word.
- Mr. Brand told us to pay attention to the meaning of the word.

Thoughts

A wonderful thing has happened because I have mentored students' interest in words. My students have become vocal about my helping them learn about important words during content curriculum studies. They want to know how to note what are important words, why they are important, and how they can figure out the meaning of these words. The first step in helping them reach their goals is to identify important words. There is an abundance of wonderful nonfiction texts that will help you think along with students about important words. One of my class's favorite books is *Roanoke: The Lost Colony.* My students enjoy the story and text features of this book.

Activity

"Important word" is an idea I plant in my students' heads on the first day of school. I try not to ask my students to independently collect important words in a curriculum content study until after this lesson. This lesson is no more than a read-aloud of *Roanoke: The Lost Colony* using the question, Why do you think the authors thought this word was important?

While I am reading aloud, my students are noting the important words in their notebooks and then thinking about why these words are important in relation to understanding the text and idea.

The students and I discuss their thinking about why each word was chosen as an important word on that page. I also ask my students to record any other words they felt were important and to note why they felt they were important. I have found that it takes me two days to get through this text.

I create an anchor chart with the students of what are important words. Then the students read independently from their social studies textbook, noting important words.

When we discuss their reading, we make a chart of important words and discuss the why of their selections.

Word Savvy: Integrated Vocabulary, Spelling, and Word Study, Grades 3–6 by Max Brand. Copyright © 2004. Stenhouse Publishers.

| # The Words of Subtitles

Materials

- Overhead transparency or chart paper
- Textbook
- Overhead copy of text
- Inquiry notebooks
- Pencils

Thoughts

I ask my students to preview textbooks prior to reading assignments. While they are previewing an assignment, I ask them to look at a variety of text features, including the subtitles. The subtitles can be confusing because of the brevity of the language used and the information that is being signaled to the reader. The vocabulary can also be confusing because of plays on words. This organizational structure works well in a textbook that covers a breadth of information, but it confuses many students. I have discovered that the dual meaning of words and the lack of context make it hard for students to read the section of text and fully comprehend the information. To help them develop previewing strategies for reading textbooks, I use this lesson exhaustively during the first semester of the school year. While the students read the text, they take discovery notes related to the ideas of the subtitles.

Activity

I like to use this lesson once my students have had experience reading *Time for Kids* articles. I begin the lesson by providing a brief overview of the information the students are going to read. We read the title and subtitles, look at the pictures, and read the captions together.

We read the subtitles together and think out loud what the information in each section could be about.

The students then read the text and take notes in their inquiry notebooks about the ideas signaled in the subtitles. I ask them to record important words that help them understand the main ideas of the text.

I position myself so I can observe students read and record notes. I like to ask them why they noted a key word, idea, or phrase in their inquiry notebooks. I may also listen to a student or two while they are silently reading to monitor fluency, accuracy, and understanding.

I bring the students together and record key words, ideas, or phrases on a chart. We use their notes to explore their thinking. If they missed something important, I will reread the text and explain my thinking.

Word Savvy: Integrated Vocabulary, Spelling, and Word Study, Grades 3–6 by Max Brand. Copyright © 2004. Stenhouse Publishers.

Learning Vocabulary Across the Curriculum

Making vocabulary study meaningful *and* useful *for students has always been the difficult part. As teachers we must help students incorporate new words into their existing language in ways that don't seem phony.*

Janet Allen (1999, 40)

Kelsey talks about unearthing her thinking. Tyler describes his journey from Atlanta, Georgia, to Dublin, Ohio, by using a word wall term, *meandering.* Brad searches for the right word to describe the euphoria of winning a baseball championship. Brienna and Drake try explaining their understanding of phases of the moon, using *waxing* and *waning* in their writing.

These are but a handful of instances where students used their developing vocabulary in a wide range of contexts. According to Beck, McKeown, and Kucan (2002), "Knowing a word is not an all-or-nothing proposition; it is not the case that one either knows or does not know a word. Rather, knowledge of a word should be viewed in terms of the extent or degree of knowledge that people can possess." When students meet new words in context and have multiple opportunities to use these words, the new words become familiar and frequently used.

Wonderful word-learning opportunities come up in content instruction. Math, social studies, and science have specific vocabularies that promote curiosity about root words, affixes, and derivations.

Developing concept knowledge is one way we can increase students' world and word knowledge. When attempting to evaluate students' understanding of vocabulary and concepts in content areas, I scour their journals, rapid writes (see Lesson 6.6), and projects, noting vocabulary use.

Teaching students to use an ever-growing lexicon in content areas takes practice, guidance, and strategic teaching. I know at the beginning of the year I grow restless when students do not use new vocabulary words that I think they should use. I have to take a step back and ask, Have I shown them how to do this? Am I using the new vocabulary? Do I encourage them to try on the new vocabulary during our conversations? Here, as with all new learning in my classroom, demonstrations are important.

I try to keep the following in mind while planning: "Learners must have access to the meaning of words [that] teachers or their surrogates (e.g., other adults, books, films) use to guide them into contemplating known concepts in novel ways (to learn something new). With inadequate vocabulary knowledge, learners are being asked to develop novel combinations of known concepts with insufficient tools" (Baker, Simmons, and Kameenui 2003, 1).

Meaningful Use

I know that the vocabulary and ideas that students are developing is complex, often just beyond their independent understanding. Terms like *segregation, patriotism, pilgrims, waxing,* and *waning* are challenging because of the ideas they convey. Classroom conversations help students see the relationships between words and ideas as they try to relate what they know to new thinking.

When we begin an investigation in math, science, or social studies, there are concepts, terms, and phrases I focus on for instruction. These learning goals come from state standards and district curriculum guides. In the exploratory stages of investigations, I try to carefully weave important vocabulary into conversations. Listening to what students are trying to say, and helping them say it using the new vocabulary, goes a long way toward helping students use target words. Semantic maps, Venn diagrams, and linear arrays (see Figure 6.1) can be constructed during conversations to help students visualize relationships between new vocabulary and their background knowledge. These visuals can be revisited as students develop awareness of emerging content concepts.

The goal of this type of instruction is providing students with strategies and tools they can use to organize their thinking, so that they can

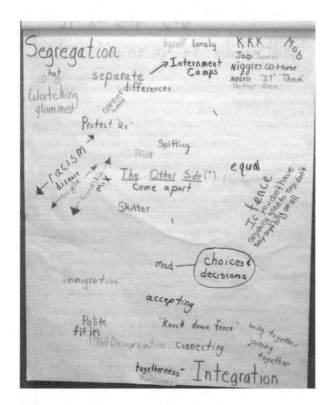

Figure 6.1 A linear array for *segregation/integration* to show the gray areas between two words with opposite meanings.

Questions posted by students about turtles. I began investigations with students' "wonders."

independently demonstrate their understanding of concepts while writing as well as during drama, readers' theater, and research projects.

I know in the past I have assigned independent projects without adequately equipping students with tools and strategies to learn from the experience. I have learned that moving slowly is critical in helping students develop independence.

I now like to launch content investigations with a discovery period. During this discovery period, students read text that builds background knowledge. Students use their inquiry notebooks to note interesting words and ideas. I guide them to use new vocabulary while developing an investigation question.

For example, during an initial science investigation, students were wondering how to determine the gender of our class turtles. During the discovery period of the investigation, the students used informational texts, the Internet, and firsthand observation to gather information and data. While conducting research, the terms *gender, bask, omnivore, carapace, scutes, clutch, hatchling, fore claws,* and *terrapin* were discovered and used. These terms became important as I helped the students become specific with their observations, questions, and learning. These words became part of the tapestry of our daily conversations and observations as we observed the behaviors and characteristics of our class turtles.

Once students have gathered information in their inquiry notebooks, I like to create class charts displaying this information (see Figure 6.2). I

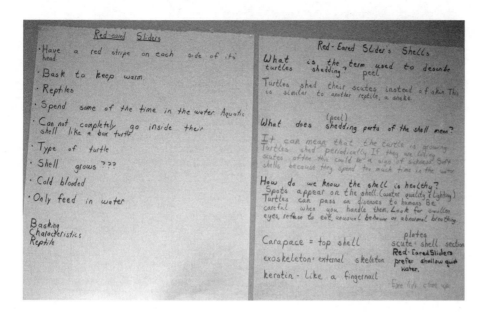

Figure 6.2 One of the many charts I used to help students organize their thinking and develop content vocabulary.

have discovered that students find ideas and words that they cannot always pronounce or understand. The class chart allows me to teach the students how to pronounce and use information they have discovered and are curious about. The chart provides me with a teaching opportunity to demonstrate how to organize notes so they can be used for observations, further inquiry, and research or project work.

I pull the group over to the corner of the room where the turtle aquarium is located. I wonder out loud, "Do you think Slider is female? She's much larger than Speedy." (The students had learned that female red-eared sliders are larger than males.) Brad answers my question with another question: "Could one of the turtles be older than the other? When did you get those turtles?" "I bought Slider about two years before I was given Speedy," I tell Brad and the group.

Joseph, who is kneeling in the first row, says, "Look at the scutes on Slider—they have rings just like a male." The group takes a hard look at the turtle's shell, trying to examine the sections of the shell they have learned are called scutes. Abby asks, "Joseph, are the claws on Slider's fore claws longer than Speedy's?" "It looks like it," Joseph responds. "I think Mr. Brand should take the turtles out of the tank so we can measure them."

"Before I do that," I say, "what else could we examine to make our inference about the gender of the turtles Speedy and Slider?" Katie guides the group by stating the now obvious, "Look at the stripe on their necks. Speedy's stripe is more of a dull orange, so it must be a she." "Slider, then, is a boy because of the bright red stripe," adds Sydney.

Student's inquiry notebook entry based on observations of the class turtle.

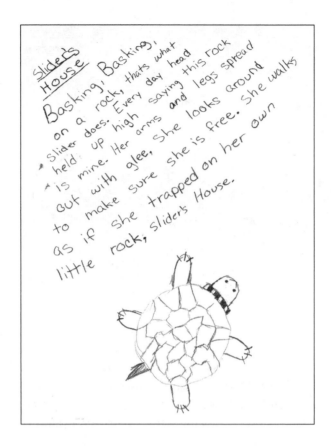

Slider's House

Basking, Basking, Basking, on a rock, that's what Slider does. Every day head held up high saying this rock is mine. Her arms and legs spread out with glee. She looks around to make sure she is free. She walks as if she trapped on her own little rock, Slider's House.

The students had an opportunity to research, discuss, observe, note, and use their growing vocabulary about turtles. I like to slowly build vocabulary during experiences that involve the students, so that the vocabulary becomes a necessary part of the discussion, experiment, or project. Intermediate-grade students like to sound grown up as they discuss their learning, so content learning is ripe with daily opportunities to create an interest in words. Students would much rather use the term *gnomon* than *sundial* to describe a shadow stick. How do I stoke this curiosity? During my daily discussions with my students, which usually are a result of something I have been reading aloud to them.

Read-aloud is the perfect place for me to begin demonstrating the thinking I want my students to do in content learning. I like using nonfiction reading materials. These texts often challenge the students because of the content and vocabulary. Typically, I'll read a short section from a nonfiction text. The section I choose to read helps answer student-initiated questions, often provoking further questions as students work to understand major concepts. The questions under investigation help shape the format the group will use to take notes.

If I introduce or use a graphic organizer, it is important to embed reasons that this graphic representation was chosen in the discussion. I also try to incorporate how this is helping me understand content and vocabulary. This is critical in teaching for independent application as I gradually relinquish responsibility to my students. If students are to use and adapt organizational strategies, this knowledge helps them during independent application. I use my notebook and chart paper during vocabulary demonstration lessons. I ask the students to use their inquiry notebooks to track their thinking and take notes.

For example, while reading about the moon during a science investigation, Morgan, Laura, Chris, Matt, and Michael came across a puzzling idea—the changing shape of the moon is an illusion. The class found this idea interesting, so I helped the group investigate this idea prior to their researching their own lunar questions.

I helped the students take this information and form it into a "wonder." The wonder question became, Does the moon change shape? This was a similar "wonder" to one the students would investigate during their own research. I chose *The Moon Book* by Gail Gibbons as a text to demonstrate note taking and inferring vocabulary. I chose this book because of the brevity and language used to explain the illusion of the moon's changing shape. The idea that the moon changes shape was new to a majority of the class. If the idea was not entirely new, the terms *waxing* and *waning* were, as an explanation for this illusion.

Reading aloud while demonstrating note taking, using a graphic organizer to help infer the meaning of new words, and writing a short response incorporating new vocabulary are all steps that I find help prepare my students for independent learning activities. I have coined the term *rapid write* for this activity (see Lesson 6.6) because once the students understand how to do this type of activity, I expect it to move quickly. Students take about five minutes to write a summary paragraph after reading a short text (which sometimes may be a textbook passage). The following goals for the rapid write activity focus my instruction:

- Read to answer a question.
- Use note taking to help shape thinking and understanding about a topic.
- Write to discover what you have learned about a topic or concept.
- Use new and important vocabulary while writing.
- Find your own nonfiction writing voice.

Prior to reading from *The Moon Book*, I tell my students, "While I'm reading, I will collect words that I think will help me understand the question about whether the moon changes shape. I am going to use my notebook to write down important ideas and vocabulary. This will help me organize my rapid write today. I want you to listen and write down vocabulary words and ideas you think will help you."

Laura asks, "Which way should we turn the page?" I respond, "Which way do you think will help you?" The students turn their notebooks, thinking carefully. I give them a minute before telling them, "I think I'll try to turn my notebook sideways so I can space out my thinking."

I do not want to make this an overwhelming task, so I try to record a few important words during the read-aloud. I jot the following vocabulary words in my notebook: *illusion, reflect, luminous, waxing,* and *waning.* Each time I wrote a word in my notebook, the students asked what I was doing. I showed them my entry while explaining my thinking, focusing on how this vocabulary helps me to better understand the illusion of the moon's changing shape.

I have found that some students are tentative while learning how to take notes. They like to wait and record only what the teacher does; they seem to want to "get it right." Others, like Laura, Kelsey, and Michael, have a page full of notes and challenge me with questions and ideas during each step of the process.

The students helped me create a semantic web in my notebook around the words *waxing* and *waning* (see Figure 6.3). After reading aloud, I recorded the word webs on a chart. These semantic webs would be used during the rapid write demonstration. The group also added ideas to the word webs during the remainder of our moon exploration study. I knew it was important for the students to understand that *waxing* means "increase" and *waning* means "decrease." The conversation, of course, needed to focus on the illusion of the moon's changing shape, which was our question for the investigation. Getting the graphic organizer on the chart paper quickly while discussing and reviewing the idea helps you maintain the students' attention as you prepare to write.

The challenge the students face is how to go from a graphic organizer to a written text. My modeled writing supported students' learning this skill. Showing students how a graphic organizer helped me to understand the question and to use the new vocabulary in my writing was critical.

Notes and graphic organizers are only tools for thinking. The ability to learn from texts using notes and organizational strategies for inferring word meanings independently is the goal. This process takes a long time, but independence is the payoff for this well-spent time.

Figure 6.4 shows Drake's rapid write after hearing about the illusion of the moon's changing shape. Rapid writes are a good assessment instrument to use when evaluating if students are learning both conceptual knowledge and vocabulary.

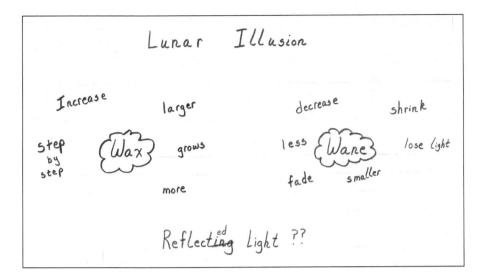

Figure 6.3 Semantic web—waxing/waning.

The writing is representative of the class. The students are developing their own nonfiction writing voice. Most of the students choose to use a question as a topic sentence. The students' writing stays focused on topic, using vocabulary that is important (*illuminate, waxing, waning*) to show what they learned. The students are learning how to embed a definition to help the reader understand important or confusing vocabulary. This

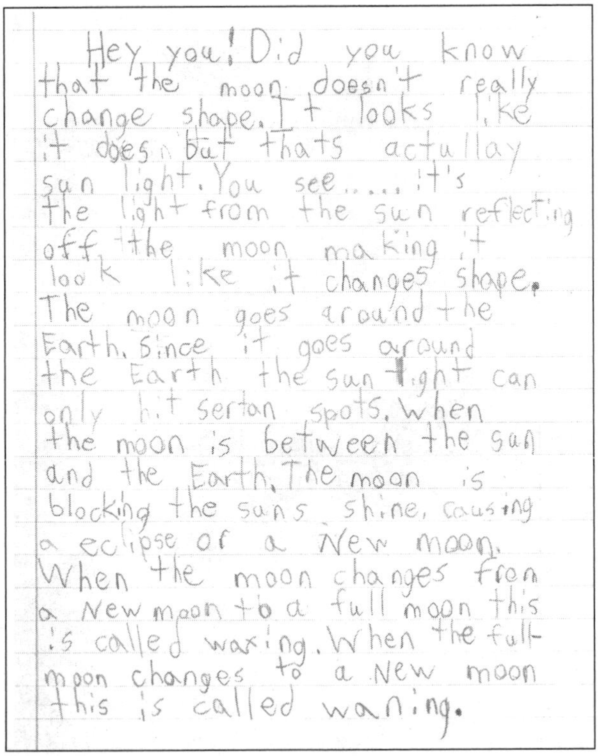

Figure 6.4 Student's rapid write about the moon.

> Hey you! Did you know that the moon doesn't really change shape. It looks like it does, but thats actullay sun light. You see..... it's the light from the sun reflecting off the moon making it look like it changes shape. The moon goes around the Earth. Since it goes around the Earth the sun light can only hit sertan spots. When the moon is between the sun and the Earth, The moon is blocking the suns shine, causing a eclipse or a New moon. When the moon changes from a New moon to a full moon this is called waxing. When the full moon changes to a New moon this is called waning.

idea takes in the notion of being aware of an audience. The first reader of a draft is the student writer, but the second reading comes from a peer, as students confer and comment prior to turning in work.

What is next? In leading the students toward independence, it is important for them to look at more nonfiction texts, exploring how authors use words and embed understanding of these words and concepts into the writing. I often approach this as an inquiry by asking students to buddy-read texts, search for new vocabulary, and note what the author is doing. The students' discoveries are used as we create anchor charts to help us think through strategies for learning and using vocabulary while writing.

Moving Toward Independence

In our class study of the Revolutionary War period, the students were having difficulty making heads or tails out of the often-heard terms *patriot* and *loyalist*. The students decided during independent reading from their social studies book and trade books that they would record ideas in their inquiry notebooks to help them organize their understanding (see Figure 6.5).

Figure 6.5 Student's *patriot* notebook page.

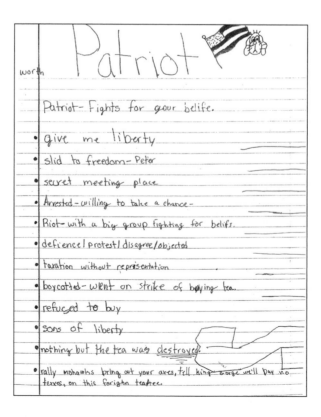

Figures 6.6 Left: Student's sketch on *whippoorwill* and Harriet Tubman. Right: Student's sketch on *rogue* and Roger Williams.

Words and lines that were used to describe patriots and loyalists were recorded. Comparing and contrasting these concepts by using students' notes helped the class develop an understanding of the two groups of colonists and their roles during this historical period. The students were beginning to take responsibility for their own learning, using a tool that I often suggested. It was important to use their notes to create a class graphic aid on chart paper to use during class discussion.

While reading biographies the students found it helpful to adapt the word sketch activity (see Lesson 3.8) as a way to organize their note taking. They recorded words and phrases that captured the essence of the individual they were reading about. They also created visual representations of the person they were researching with descriptors highlighting their sketches (see Figure 6.6). In the poem "Whippoorwill," Beverly McLoughland's (1999) choice of *whippoorwill* to describe Harriet Tubman led us down the path of how to use context to infer the relationship to a bird. The children found additional meaning when they broke the word into parts, *whip-poor-will.*

Chris had an interesting way of organizing his description of Roger Williams after reading Amy Allison's *Roger Williams, Founder of Rhode Island. Rogue* became a frequently used word, and the students became independent in their use of this complex vocabulary word. These notes developed into a prewriting activity in which students wrote biographical sketches about important Americans.

An ABC Project

Learning about colonial times presented the students with many opportunities to use vocabulary strategies independently as they tried to make sense of this important period of American history. I suggested we create a class ABC book as a culminating project for our studies. The kids thought this would be an easy way to demonstrate what they had learned during the winter months.

The class revised my idea, saying they would like to create a collage of connected thoughts that would become a tapestry to hang outside our classroom. This would allow the outside world of the school to get a glimpse into what our class had been learning and thinking about during the snowy winter, when they did not have much contact with schoolmates because of inside recess.

Thinking about the learning the kids would have to accomplish during this project, I listed the following goals:

- Understand colonial times, including the French and Indian War, British acts and taxes, Boston Tea Party, Boston Massacre, First Continental Congress, and other related historical events.
- Learn vocabulary that describes and was used during this time period.
- Create a list of words that begin with each letter by using what is in students' thoughts and digging into trade books and textbooks.
- Reflect upon the list of words, thinking about creating an image with these words that represents colonial times.
- Use words and a text structure to create an image that represents an important part of colonial times.

We began the project by reading a variety of ABC books.

Intriguing Alphabet Books for Older Readers
A Is for America Devin Scillian
A Is for Asia by Cynthia Chin-Lee
B Is for Buckeye: An Ohio Alphabet by Marcia Schonberg
G Is for Googol: A Math Alphabet Book by David Schwartz

Figure 6.7 *ABC of Colonial Times* sample page.

K Is for Kwanza by Juwanda G. Ford
Z Is for Zamboni: A Hockey Alphabet by Matt Napier
The Z Was Zapped by Chris Van Allsburg
The Absolutely Awful Alphabet by Mordicai Gerstein
Many Nations: An Alphabet of Native America by Joseph Bruchac

Michael and Chris liked the format and style of *Z Is for Zamboni*. Melissa and Katie thought *B Is for Buckeye* would be a wise choice because the theme was familiar. The class liked the format of both books because rhymes and rhythm were used on the left-hand page and the explanation of the vocabulary was given on the right-hand page. It was agreed that this would be the format we would attempt to replicate.

Students worked in pairs and individually (depending on their preference), collecting words for a particular letter. The students enjoyed this time, as they reread trade books and their social studies textbook with their eyes on important time period words. The students swapped words like baseball cards, trying to create a list of approximately twenty words to whittle down into rhymes.

Sorting through a list of words to create a rhythm and rhymes that make sense was a bit more challenging than they had thought. Once Michael, Chris, Joseph, Abby, and Sydney got their first drafts finished, the others started to get the hang of the process. After a week of writing, revising, and agreeing and disagreeing on such important details as beats per line and whether rhyme was important, the tapestry/big book was complete.

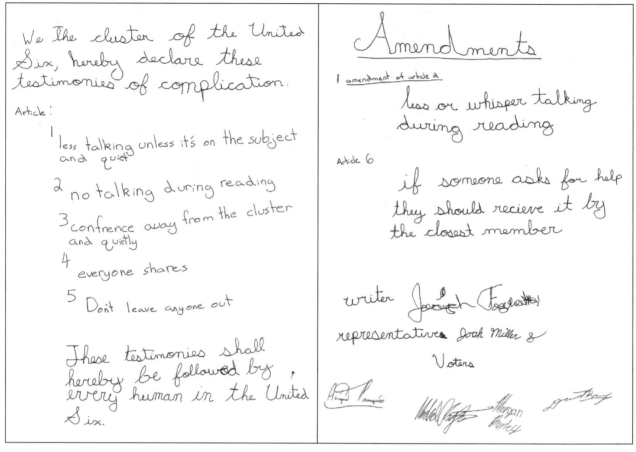

We The cluster of the United Six, hereby declare these testimonies of complication.

Article:

1 less talking unless it's on the subject and quiet

2 no talking during reading

3 confrence away from the cluster and quietly

4 everyone shares

5 Don't leave anyone out

These testimonies shall hereby be followed by , every human in the United Six.

Amendments

1 amendment of article a
less or whisper talking during reading

Article 6
if someone asks for help they should recieve it by the closest member

writer Joseph
representatives Josh Miller &
Voters

Figure 6.8 Cluster of United Six writing sample.

The students learned the research and writing process from the inside out as they assembled this *ABC of Colonial Times* book (see Figure 6.7). The students had to negotiate not only with a partner but with the entire class as they revised their thinking along the way. The project forced students to dig deeply into the meaning of the vocabulary words they picked up during the colonial times investigation.

Word-Rich Concepts

Students develop vocabulary as they have opportunities to use new terms to explain developing concepts in meaningful ways. I have found that students need to develop strategies to infer word meaning and use them during conversations, while writing, and when completing projects.

The Cluster of the United Six's writing (see Figure 6.8) reminds me of the importance of developing and using vocabulary in meaningful ways. For this project, we spent time studying the language of the U.S.

Constitution, picking out important and interesting words. We talked about the meaning of these words. Then we dramatized the Constitutional Convention, role playing and using this language. I tried to push my students to sound like the creators of the Constitution.

Vocabulary knowledge is at the heart of developing understanding of new ideas and concepts. Students need to build new vocabulary so they can understand ideas they encounter at school, through peer interactions, and in texts. Students' vocabulary size and use has often been correlated to school achievement. My goal is to make students' vocabulary rich by demonstrating and by guiding them to savor, collect, and use words. While they are collecting words, I teach them how to use the context of a word or a graphic representation to help them infer the meaning of the word.

Vocabulary-rich students also need opportunities to use the words in meaningful contexts. While students are test-driving these words, I have found it important to provide feedback that demonstrates how to use the words. One of the ways I have found to interest my students in words is to use the walls of my classroom to display words, phrases, and sentences they discover. Chapter 7 explains how I organize my wall spaces to support students' vocabulary and spelling knowledge.

Vocabulary and Schema Preview

Materials

- Short text like "Whiteout"
- Overhead transparency of text
- Overhead transparency or chart paper (optional)

Vocabulary Discussed While Reading "Whiteout"

skillet

"the slickest of sleds"

blanketed

northeaster

"blizzard-force winds"

snow-weary

mere

Thoughts

One morning Tyler caught me off guard by telling me he had been taking karate lessons. He demonstrated his karate stance along with his primordial scream. Tyler told me, "The karate stance is critical to a good lesson because I get in the proper frame of mind. I clear my head and focus on karate." Similarly, taking a stance toward reading is critical for the reader. Proficient readers take a stance toward the text they are going to read by asking themselves questions that activate prior knowledge and schema. I like to help students develop this habit by using information in the text that they may not focus on. I preview the text, asking myself questions. I often ask questions about the types of words an author may have used while writing about a specific topic. Titles, subtitles, headings, captions, photographs, illustrations, and sidebars are resources students may not have previewed in depth.

Activity

I begin by telling the students, "We are going to read about a blizzard that caused many cities to shut down." I pass out the text, "Whiteout."

I begin previewing by thinking out loud: "Whiteout. Wow, that must have been some blizzard. I wonder if this was the worst storm ever to have hit the East Coast." I read the subtitle: "'The blizzard of '96 blanketed the East and stopped ordinary life in its tracks.' Hmm, stopped ordinary life. What is this about?"

I look at the picture and notice the Capitol in the background and wonder, "It must have something about sledding. It would be neat to sled down Capitol Hill."

I read through each subtitle, thinking out loud about what information might be in each section. I reflect on why I think the author chose the words for each subtitle. I also predict words and information that may be included in each section.

While reading the text, I discuss how previewing helped me think about what I was going to read.

After the reading, we discuss the benefits of previewing and taking a stance toward the text that will be read. Students share how they will incorporate this strategy into their everyday reading.

Word Savvy: Integrated Vocabulary, Spelling, and Word Study, Grades 3–6 by Max Brand. Copyright © 2004. Stenhouse Publishers.

Use the Clues to Infer Meaning

Materials

- Short text like "Saving Our National Parks": "Part of the problem is the many people who camp in the parks. This glut of tourists is choking the parks with cars that cause pollution and run over animals."
- Overhead transparency of text
- Overhead transparency or chart paper

Vocabulary Discussed While Reading "Saving Our National Parks"

This list represents the words chosen by students in my class. Surprisingly, all the children did not understand the word *glut*. Since all the children did not understand this word, I used it as the demonstration word.

oasis

grave

glut

preserves

nearsighted

conjunction

Word Savvy: Integrated Vocabulary, Spelling, and Word Study, Grades 3–6 by Max Brand. Copyright © 2004. Stenhouse Publishers.

Thoughts

Words and their meanings are the marrow of my thinking about words with my students. Students have a certain degree of difficulty inferring meaning of words, especially while reading content area or nonfiction materials. To guide my students' thinking about how to use contextual support while they are reading, I periodically use this lesson. During this process it is important to demonstrate the importance of monitoring what the reader already understands about the text being read and where the reader's understanding of the text stops. Once I have worked through this process with my students, I model how I reread with a specific purpose in mind. This lesson works well with small groups of students prior to their own silent reading of textbooks, articles, or nonfiction trade books.

Activity

I like to use this lesson during the first or second week of school. I begin by providing a brief overview of the article the students are going to read. We read the title and subtitles, look at the pictures, and read the captions together.

I explain what an editorial is and what they can expect to find out. Then I instruct the students to read the article twice.

The first reading focuses the students' attention on the main idea and sentences that support it. To help them, they underline important words, phrases, and sentences that the editor used to make the point of the article. On the second reading, the students highlight words that are confusing.

I position myself so I can observe students read, underline, and highlight the article. I may also listen to a student or two while they are silently reading to monitor fluency, accuracy, and understanding.

I chart all words students have found confusing or difficult. I ask if they had heard the word prior to their reading. This is a great assessment tool.

In this situation we all went back and located the word *glut*. We reread the sentence together. Since the word was at the beginning of the sentence, I suggested that it might be important to go back and reread the preceding sentence. This time we reread through both sentences. I then demonstrated my thinking about how I used information from both sentences. I tell students how *many people* and *glut* go with the illustration. I can see that there are a lot of people in a small area and that this is causing pollution. Now in my head, when I think of the word *glut*, it means many things grouped together in a small area.

Materials

- Overhead transparency or chart paper
- Nonfiction text
- Teacher's overhead of text
- Selected picture books
- Word study notebooks
- Pencils

Words Collected While Studying Persuasive Writing

This list is not exhaustive and will be added to during the year.

imagine

in addition

think of

after all

another reason

according to

why does

how will

pluses

minuses

my view

need

should

want

vital

benefit

Thoughts

One of the difficulties my students had while writing the variety of genres required over the course of the school year was lack of genre-specific writing vocabulary. To help them develop genre-specific writing vocabularies, I had them read and note words used by authors writing the type of text I was focusing my instruction on. I decided to extend this thinking to developing vocabulary by asking them to note not only the form used and its function but the words, sentence patterns, and purposes they serve. Normally, the students will read three or four short articles or pieces of text as an introduction to the writing genre study. *Time for Kids,* other periodicals, and picture books are great models because students can envision themselves writing similar texts. My goal is for students to see patterns of specific words that are used in a genre as they develop oral and written vocabularies.

Activity

I like to begin a writing genre by studying texts. About a week before asking students to write in a selected genre, I read aloud and use shared reading to model a form of writing.

During the shared reading of a text, I ask students to note specific vocabulary. Students record this in their word study notebooks.

Students read the selected text silently. I discuss the article with them. Then I ask the students to go back and notice the words the author used that they feel are specific to this genre. When they notice a word, I ask them to record it in their word study notebooks.

While the students are rereading the article, I move around the room and observe and confer with the students. The conversation during the reflection session is richer if I have worked with a few of the students.

Once the students have completed their second reading, noticing and noting words, I chart the words on chart paper or an overhead transparency. I discuss the students' decision and thoughts. I find that reflective conversation is the biggest aid to transferring this thinking to independent work.

Webbing Word Meanings

Materials

- Overhead transparency or chart paper
- Inquiry notebooks
- Pencils

Words Generated Around the Key Word *Friction*

hot

grip

traction

brake

stop

slide

decelerate

skid

speed bump

rubbing object

rough

scratching

itching

static field

Thoughts

I have learned from my students that they like to learn new vocabulary words. They believe that the new vocabulary they learn makes them sound more grown up and smarter. I have found that while students are developing this new vocabulary, they are also learning essential concepts in math, science, and social studies. The word webbing I do with my students helps them connect their background knowledge, including words, to the new concept. These word webs hang on the classroom wall as a record of what we are learning and as a tool to help students grow in their vocabulary development. Most investigations I explore with my class have a few key vocabulary words. My students also keep these word webs in their inquiry notebooks so they can add to them independently while reading, researching, or conducting experiments. My goal is to help my students develop a tool for learning vocabulary.

Activity

I like to begin a content curriculum investigation with this activity. My students have their inquiry notebooks with them so they can copy the word web into their notebooks. I write a key word in the center of a piece of chart paper (*friction*). I read the word and tell the class, "This is a big idea that we are going to explore for the next few weeks. We are going to keep track of words that help us understand *friction*."

I then ask, "When you hear the word *friction*, what words come to mind?" I chart the students' responses.

I remind the students, "During our investigation of *friction*, while you are reading, researching, or conducting experiments and discover words that help you understand *friction*, record them on your *friction* word web."

Each day during the discussion segment of a curriculum investigation, I ask students if they have discovered any words that we need to add to the class word web. This discussion helps me to assess whether students are learning what I had planned. If students do not come up with ideas, I prompt them to rethink about their reading or steps they took during an activity or experiment.

The discussion section of a lesson helps my students become responsible for keeping track of what they are learning and provides me with information for further instruction.

Word Savvy: Integrated Vocabulary, Spelling, and Word Study, Grades 3–6 by Max Brand. Copyright © 2004. Stenhouse Publishers.

135

| # What Is Key?

Materials

- Chart paper
- Textbook or short nonfiction text
- Inquiry notebooks
- Pencils

Thoughts

Helping students identify key information in oral language and written texts is a skill many intermediate-grade students need help with. I have found that while students read nonfiction texts, especially textbooks, they have trouble locating key information. Thinking along and guiding students toward key words is important. Students who learn how to identify key words and ideas understand the texts they read and learn from those experiences. Teaching students previewing strategies and how to think about purposes for reading the text helps them locate key words and information.

Activity

I like to use this lesson at the beginning of the year when I am introducing my students to textbook reading. I prepare the students to read the text by prompting them to look at the title, subtitles, pictures, captions, and other text features of a short section of their textbook.

I ask my students to write in their inquiry notebooks what they think their reading will teach them. While they are writing their thoughts, I move around the room, reading their thoughts and guiding their thinking.

I think along with my students and record their thoughts on a piece of chart paper. (My students have grown accustomed to adding information I record on the chart that they did not include.) I demonstrate how this thinking will shape how I read this text.

The students read the text and record key words and ideas in their inquiry notebooks.

I position myself so I can observe students read, underline, and highlight the text. I may also listen to a student or two while they are silently reading to monitor fluency, accuracy, and understanding.

I chart all the words and ideas students found that they thought were key. We discuss why these words and ideas are important. Then we use shared writing to summarize our reading, trying to include the key words and ideas.

Word Savvy: Integrated Vocabulary, Spelling, and Word Study, Grades 3–6 by Max Brand. Copyright © 2004. Stenhouse Publishers.

Materials

- Overhead transparency or chart paper
- Nonfiction text
- Notebook paper
- Inquiry notebooks
- Pencils

Important Information to Include in Rapid Writes

- Complete sentences
- Key vocabulary used correctly or explained
- Capitalization
- Important ideas explained
- Paragraphs

Once Students Are Efficient Rapid Writers

- Reread
- Underline spelling errors
- Have a Go on spelling errors
- Have someone read

Thoughts

I like to help my students summarize what they have learned after reading nonfiction, watching a video, or hearing a speaker. Since my students take notes, I want them to learn how to take information from their notes and transfer it to their writing and thinking. This five-minute writing has helped my students not only become fluent with their writing and thinking but also pay close attention to their reading, videos, or oral presentations. I help my students include key vocabulary in their writing and thinking. This helps me assess my students' understanding of content area material. Once my students get the hang of this short activity, we develop an anchor chart of information that should be included in a rapid write. Over the years my students have enjoyed this type of writing as they have learned how to craft thoughtful paragraphs that include important information, including new vocabulary. Rapid writes are also a good resource to help students locate and edit spelling errors.

Activity

Once my students are comfortable taking discovery notes (see Lesson 5.3), I introduce the rapid write. I ask my students to bring their nonfiction text and inquiry notebooks with them as we assemble in front of a chart. The chart has my notes written for the students to review, challenge, or question.

I then think aloud about my notes, focusing on discoveries, questions answered, and key words. I begin to orally start crafting what I have learned from my reading.

Next, I write quickly in front of my students. I ask the students to watch what I do during this demonstration writing.

The students typically comment on how quickly I wrote, that I used many of the ideas from my notes and what I had told them I was thinking. The big thing they notice is that once I started writing, I did not stop. The writing flows from one idea to the next.

I then ask my students to go back to their seats and take a moment to look over their notes to prepare to do a rapid write. I warn them that they may not finish in five minutes. That is all right. They will learn, and by the end of the week, the students do finish up in a short time period.

Simile Sort

Materials

- Wall of phrases and sentences

Interesting Similes

"like peeking under a Band-Aid at a scrape"

"like a horse's patootie"

"ugly as sin"

"as mad as flies in a fruit jar"

Thoughts

I know that while I read, my notebook is close at hand. I use my notebook to store the wonderful sentences, phrases, sayings, and words that grab my attention. I ask my students to do the same thing in their reading logs. Students then copy some of the wonderful language onto sentence strips for their classmates to marvel at. I notice that my students are often enraptured by similes. It must be the play with language used to create these catchy comparisons. Once I notice a number of similes on the wall, I teach the students what a simile is and rearrange the wall so that we can keep the similes together.

Activity

The simile sort is an easy way to launch a dialogue and exploration about similes. I tell my students, "I notice that you have been collecting a lot of phrases from your reading that have interesting comparisons." I point to a few of the similes on the wall. "This type of comparison is called a simile.

"One of the things I notice about the similes you have collected is that they seem to use the word *like* or *as* to emphasize the comparison," I say. Lots of nodding heads and rereading, and some students trying to recall what they had been taught about similes.

I then take the similes off the wall and begin a new column for students to post them.

I have found that students try writing similes in their own writing notebooks after this lesson. I use the classroom door to post the students' creations. Students playing with similes seem to be more thoughtful in their writing once I begin sorting similes out and give them a name.

Building Walls
of Words

If we hope to write well, we have to learn from the men and women who have mastered our craft. We draw as close to them as they will allow and watch them at work. This is apprenticeship the old-fashioned way and I don't believe there's any way around it. We need to read and reread the finest writers we can find. We need to study and savor their language. And on occasion we might copy snatches of it into a notebook as a reminder of what language can do in the hands of a skilled writer.

Ralph Fletcher (1996, 40)

Words have adorned the walls of my classroom in one form or another during my entire teaching career. These walls of words have taken on a life of their own, as my students have helped me construct and revise my thinking about word walls.

Each August I sit in my classroom meeting area plotting the purpose and placement of word walls. My thinking begins with reflection: How did last year's word wall support the students' word-learning needs? I think through how students learned high-frequency words, became fluent using generative spelling strategies, and developed strategies for learning vocabulary, and most important, how having a word wall enhanced writing.

If I am thinking about displaying words, Janet Allen's (1999) advice is important: "We need to have the words in full view so that the students can see them and use them in their writing" (70). For me the largest wall is the best choice because all the desks are clustered in this area. I consider the following purposes for having a word wall.

Purposes for a Word Wall
- Support students' learning of high-frequency words
- Provide example words highlighting difficult concepts as a help to students when spelling unfamiliar words
- Support students' vocabulary development
- Demonstrate how to collect words found during reading
- Provide a space for students to display words that are important to them
- Provide a space for students to sort and categorize words and phrases

These are the reasons I devote a large portion of my classroom wall space to displaying words. Depending on the grade level that I am teaching, I have to sort through this list, prioritizing my purposes. I am very careful with how much wall space I use for specific purposes. I try to treat the classroom like an artist's studio, allowing work to be displayed during different stages of development.

Students need to display work in progress as they consider revisions, along with their finished projects. The classroom belongs to the students, and their voices should be heard. Once I have allocated my word wall space and prioritized my rationale for having a word wall, I consider the following organizational questions:

Will the words be displayed in alphabetical order?
What type of material will I use to mount words?
How big will the words be?
Who will be responsible for writing and hanging the words on the wall?
How long will words hang on the wall?
What criteria will be used for removing words from the wall?

Frequently Used Words

No matter how I answer the previous questions, the students enter a classroom with bare walls. This may sound unattractive, but family pictures, a rocking chair, book displays, and a pet turtle provide a homelike feeling. I know that when we first moved into our house, we lived in it a while before hanging our pictures.

If students inquire about the lack of wall hangings, I respond by asking, "What do you think should go there?" Students have a variety of responses, which give options I may not have considered. The walls fill very quickly during the first days of school as students create, revise, and paint self-portraits. The walls also fill with artistically decorated names from Name Sort (see Lesson 3.4). These activities help students pay attention to the evolving wall displays as they become responsible for the construction of the work on the walls.

Those perplexing word study questions Where should I begin? How quickly should I move? and When will I see results? have followed me to my word wall thinking. I know that my word wall thinking began with systematically introducing high-frequency words and displaying them on a large bulletin board in alphabetical order. Students need to learn to spell high-frequency words correctly in their writing. Word walls support students' correct spelling of high-frequency words.

I do not want the word wall to become a crutch for correct spelling of frequently used words. My goal is that students learn to look systematically at print as they develop strategies for learning and remembering words. Many of the frequently used words in the intermediate grades come from content area materials. I have included in the Appendix a list of words students frequently use and misspell. High-frequency words are also an objective on my state's (Ohio) English Language Arts Standards.

Spelling Goals for High-Frequency Words

Third Grade	Spell correctly all familiar high-frequency words and words with short vowels and common endings.
Fourth Grade	Spell high-frequency words correctly.
Fifth Grade	Spell high-frequency words correctly.
Sixth Grade	Spell correctly words often misspelled and high-frequency words.

The word wall has been a tool that helps students learn to spell high-frequency words and also provides me with opportunities to support development in monitoring and self-correction strategies, along with dictionary skills. My teaching bag of tricks includes a few prompts that help students remember to use the word wall without detracting from fluency while writing. These prompts help me support students' spelling and monitoring strategies. I use these prompts to help students locate a misspelled word on the word wall and correct the spelling.

Word Wall Prompts

"Reread this sentence and find the word you misspelled."
"Look at the word wall and check your spelling."
"What part of the word did you misspell?"
"What do you need to remember about the spelling of ——?"
"How do you spell ——?"
"Can you find ——?"
"How did you spell ——?"

When interacting with students using these prompts, I normally pick one misspelled word that appears on the wall. These interactions are quick and usually occur while conferring with students during content area writing. If a student has many misspelled high-frequency words, I may ask him to go through the same procedure for each, searching for the correct spelling on the word wall. Once students learn these procedures, I leave them to find and correct errors while conferring with other students. I then return and inquire what they have learned about spelling misspelled words as well as about themselves as spellers.

Reflecting on the amount of wall space needed for this type of teaching and the number of students it has affected, I've rethought my use of wall space. Most of my students had developed a system for remembering how words (including high-frequency words) are spelled. They had the ability to detect and correct spelling errors during editing and revision rereads. They understood the importance of being courteous to their readers by using conventional spelling. I became bothered by the amount of wall space I had monopolized with the lists of frequently misspelled words.

Most of the best ideas that emerge from my classroom are the result of a collaborative process, as my students and I deal with problems and come up with solutions. This makes sense because they are the ones who have to learn using the resources and materials in the learning environment. Matt's suggestion of using the cupboard door for high-frequency words made perfect sense. This was dead space, not large enough for any student work yet within eyesight of all the students' desks. Nick and Jackie moved their seats closer to this space because they used these words consistently to check on their spelling.

Students were also still having difficulty with homophones, misusing *their* and *there, right* and *write, no* and *know.* Michael and Matt (the master culprits) insisted that they knew how to spell the words correctly but not when to use each word.

This led to the creation of two anchor charts in which the homophones were used in sentences correctly (see Figure 7.1). These charts were constructed using shared writing, adding a touch of humor so that

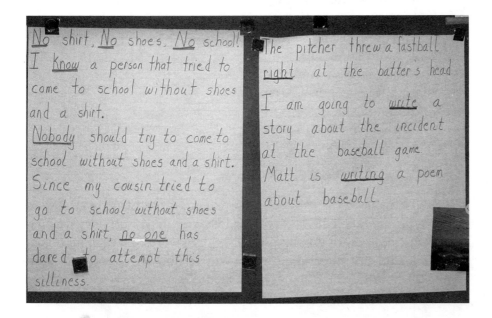

Figure 7.1 Anchor charts displaying homophones.

the students would reread and use them. The charts helped clarify the students' confusion as they learned the importance of meaning in their spelling development.

Interesting Words

Having more space to display words changed my thinking about words on the wall. My thinking shifted toward getting students to notice and wonder about words. I began to think about my notebook and the myriad of words that I collect. While reading for a variety of reasons from a variety of texts, I collect an assortment of words.

The students were always asking to look inside my notebook, so why not let them? I wanted to find a way to use the walls to help them peek not only into my notebook but into their classmates' thinking about words. I decided we would create a "collective writer's notebook" with some of our wall space. The challenge, of course, would be how to use this collective writer's notebook to stretch the students' thinking, get them to reread and reflect about these words, and envision using these words in their oral and written discourse.

I wanted students to ponder the meaning of these words, how the author's use of these words affected them as readers, and what plans they might have for the words. While rereading my writing notebook and searching for focus lesson ideas, I discovered a variety of word categories.

Word Categories
- Interesting-sounding words
- Unfamiliar words
- Words that make you stop and think
- Words I want to say over and over
- Words that have pronunciation guides
- Words that have unusual spellings
- Words that are long
- Words whose meaning I can't discern
- Words from other languages
- Words I want to use in my writing

This list helped me envision the curriculum for constructing the word wall. We would take baby steps, word by word, building understanding of the why and how of building a class wall of words. I settled on a goal of getting students interested in words. Interesting Words sounded right as one title for the wall, as I prepared to introduce this new way of thinking while reading aloud to my students.

Choosing a book for introducing this concept was a struggle. Fortunately, I had just finished reading *The Van Gogh Café* by Cynthia Rylant, so I decided I would use a picture book while introducing the idea of interesting words.

The book *Baseball Saved Us* by Ken Mochizuki was also a logical choice for me. I knew that in the author's note was *internment camp,* describing the place used to detain Japanese-Americans during World War II. This word was interesting to me, and I knew it would grab the attention of my class because we had previously read *Home of the Brave* by Allen Say, which also deals with camps used to segregate and protect American citizens.

While the class fumbled with their reading notebooks, organizing the next clean page to take notes, I interrupted them: "Today, while we are reading, I want you to write down words you think are interesting. I want you to try doing what I have shown you with my notebook and start to gather words that interest you. We are going to use the wall to keep track of the words that you find interesting. We are going to turn the wall into a class writer's notebook."

I introduce the book *Baseball Saved Us* by reading the title and wondering aloud what the book might be about. The students start writing predictions in their reading notebooks. Most students use the front cover picture and the title while constructing a prediction for this story. Josh wonders, "How can baseball save people?" He writes his question down in his notebook. Sydney responds, "Josh, I think baseball saves them from boredom. It looks like they're in jail. They need to do something, so it must be baseball." I sit back and think about how independent they are.

I continue: "This book is different than others we have read because it has an author's note, which will give us background knowledge that we can use to think about the story." I begin to read the author's note, utter *internment,* and immediately Melissa says, "Wow, like *Home of the Brave.* That's what you call those places." Tyler asks, "How do you spell *internment*? I want to put that in my notebook. Very interesting." I ask, "How do you think you spell it?" Jackie lets the group know that it sounds long and has three or four syllables. I repeat *internment,* stressing each syllable. "It has three syllables," Jackie confirms for the group. The students direct me toward the correct spelling as I record their attempts on a dry-erase board. Most of the students copy the word correctly into their reading notebooks.

I continue reading *Baseball Saved Us,* and the conversation shifts to understanding what *internment* means as well as why the government would do such a thing. After the read-aloud I challenge the students to make a column in their reading logs titled Interesting Words. While I

Figure 7.2 Interesting words discovered by students during class read-alouds and independent reading.

confer with students today, I will ask if they are discovering any interesting words. During our reflection following silent reading, I make a chart of the words the students collected. The students have noted and collected an interesting group of words, which will become part of our word wall.

Figure 7.2 shows the first collection of words that students found interesting during class read-aloud and their independent reading. The students felt at this point that they needed to create criteria for displaying words—the type of words to be added or deleted as well as including a definition.

Lines That Stick in the Mind

The following day I had to be more specific with the reason for noticing interesting words. I told the students, "Today while you are listening to *The Other Side* by Jacqueline Woodson, I want you to notice words that are interesting because of the way the author used them. They might be familiar words that are used in an unusual way. They might be words that help you understand a part of the story. Or words that you have not heard before and think are important in helping you understand the story."

Abby in her thoughtful way whispered to Morgan, "What about those lines that stick with me? Did he forget that?" I asked Morgan to share Abby's thinking, and it took us back to some of the first headings

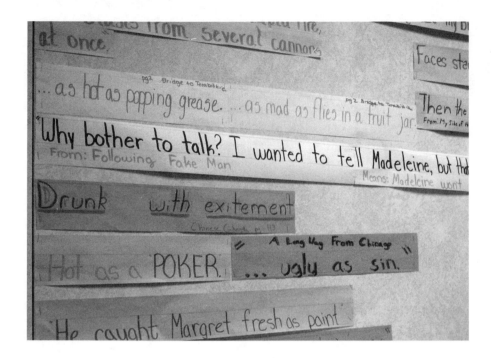

Similes gathered by the class and displayed.

for the word walls, which we had linked to poetry. Abby had reminded me of the importance of the first two months of school, as we inquired about lines of poetry—thinking through the poet's intention and use of words.

The group felt that thinking about words within sentences and phrases would help them understand the story and develop an eye for words. This felt more natural to them, and was very similar to my own word tracking in my writing notebook.

Students become responsible for collecting, recording, and managing the words and phrases on the wall. I have found that teaching students the purpose for a task, how to accomplish the task, and then allowing them to be responsible goes a long way toward independent application.

My students created criteria for display selections and designs even more rigorous than those I might have thought of. Words needed to have definitions, and lines, sentences, or phrases needed to include the book and page number.

Student Criteria for Words on the Wall
- Use your best handwriting.
- The words should be large enough to be read while sitting anywhere in the classroom.
- Include your definition for the word.
- Use quotation marks.
- Include the source and page number of your word, phrase, or quote.

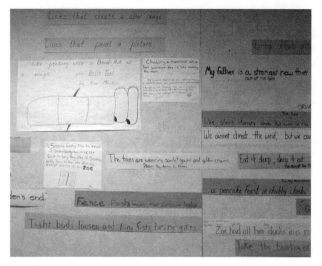

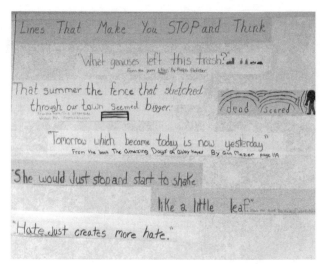

Left: Lines chosen by students for the word wall. Right: "Lines that make you stop and think."

- Choose ideas that will stretch the class's thinking.
- Do your best.

The students sometimes found these categories restrictive, so they created additional categories like "words I don't understand that sound important," "lines that paint a clear picture," and "lines that make you stop and think."

These categories helped the students while reading. They became more thoughtful about words and how they affected them as readers, especially stretching their understanding of the text. This word learning transferred to writing. The students listened to their peers writing with an ear toward words, especially words that created a picture in the reader's mind.

The students pushed each other to revise their writing, searching for words on the wall, in their notebooks, and thesauruses to match the writer's idea, understanding, and image. Chris's thoughts summarize what many students learned from collecting and thinking about words: "Collecting words helps me as a writer to be more specific in my words, and if I find something good in the book, I write it down. Maybe later I might use it in my own writing. It helps me as a reader by making me stop at parts I don't get. I reread them and that helps me understand the book better than I do now."

These are the final categories the class used to sort and categorize words, phrases, and sentences:

- Interesting words
- Words that roll off the tongue
- Zinkoff words—words that are silly
- Made-up words

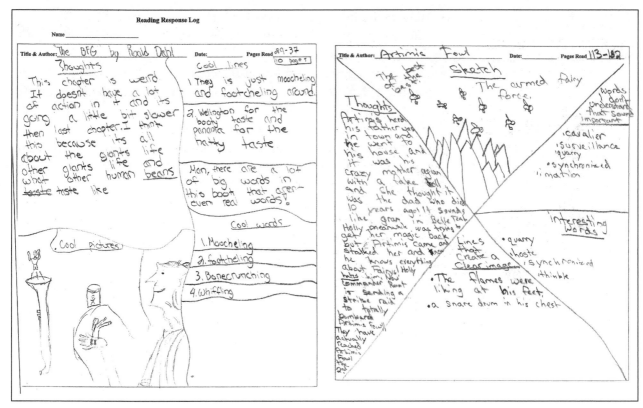

Figure 7.3 Pages from student's reading log.

- Words I don't understand
- Words that make me stop and think
- Words that are important
- Cool words
- Why did the author use that word?

Two pages from Matt's reading log (see Figure 7.3) show a student's thinking in an attempt to understand a text. This organization is connected to the words on the wall and demonstrates the effect of a word wall on the students' thinking and writing.

Thinking through the transition from having a word wall for high-frequency words to a collective writer's notebook on the wall, I saw that my students had become word-savvy. Students played an active role as they became responsible not only for collecting words but also for displaying the words on the wall. Reflecting on the usefulness of the words on the wall, I asked myself, What did the students learn? I felt the students had learned the following skills:

- Strategies for copying and remembering how to spell unfamiliar words

- How to cite information from a text
- Inferring the meaning of unfamiliar words
- Collecting words
- Envisioning possibilities for future work
- Thinking through the author's use of words, phrases, and sentences

More important, through the variety of words and writing on the wall, the students had developed into a community of learners who were interested in words. Words became a tool that helped them dig deeply while considering the meaning of a text. Words also became a tool that the students used to clarify their thinking. Chris's poem is an example of a student's final draft that began as a notebook entry and developed as he moved words and lines around, trying to express his ideas.

Nighttime
The sky is dark holding no moon or stars,
Just a vast blanket of darkness
covering everything the eye can see.

Lightning bugs fly in the pasture
giving the only light
which lights up the trees
like a Christmas tree on Christmas Eve.

Animals roam in fields
playing their nighttime games
while sly raccoons glide through the night
like bandits sneaking through loot.

Night turns to dawn,
Dawn turns to day,
Nocturnes sleep
other animals play.

By opening up our notebooks and thinking about words and displaying them on the wall, students learned to watch, listen, and talk more carefully about words in their reading and writing.

| # Homophone Anchor Chart

Materials
- Chart paper
- Homophones list

Confusing Homophones

no/know
there/their/they're
right/write
hole/whole
grate/great
principal/principle
peddle/petal/pedal
capitol/capital
pore/pour

Common Misuses

its/it's
lay/lie

Thoughts

Reading one student paper after another in which students wrote *there* for *their* or *right* for *write* bothered me. During a study of homophones, I asked the students what made these words so difficult for them. They responded by saying that they knew how to spell the words correctly but were not always sure of usage. They asked if we could create an anchor chart to help them remember the usage of homophones that they often misused. This lesson is a result of that conversation. It is important that the students help construct these charts. The humorous touches they provide make these charts a success.

Activity

The lesson begins with the students and me clustered around the chart stand. I tell the students that while reading their writing I have noticed they have had difficulties knowing when to use a particular homophone. I tell them the homophone pair.

We begin to brainstorm sentences that will help them know when to use confusing homophones.

I write the sentences on a chart. I typically underline the homophone in the sentence so that the students can quickly identify the proper word and usage.

This chart hangs in a spot in my classroom where all the students can see it while writing. I usually leave the chart up for three or four weeks because my goal is for the students to become automatic with this knowledge.

A student who may be having difficulty with homophones may copy the class sentences or their own sentences onto the last page of her word study notebook.

Word Savvy: Integrated Vocabulary, Spelling, and Word Study, Grades 3–6 by Max Brand. Copyright © 2004. Stenhouse Publishers.

| # Parts-of-Speech Sort

Materials

- Chart paper
- Words on wall
- Writing notebooks
- Pencils

Categorizing Words by Parts of Speech

The students do not have a hard time telling me that a noun is a person, place, or thing, or the object of a sentence. They are well versed in this. Verbs are what they seem to collect a lot of because they are interested in the part of the sentence that moves it along—the power part of writing. Adverbs become a bit more confusing because they are part of the prepositional phrase and work with the verb. Then there are adjectives, those descriptive words. The key is to get the students to understand how the parts of speech improve the writing so that they use this learning in their own writing.

Thoughts

I am a word collector. I collect words in my notebook for a variety of reasons. Words that I collect help stretch my vocabulary. They hibernate in my notebook, waiting for the right occasion to use them. I know I had a difficult time in school learning the parts of speech, especially distinguishing verbs, adverbs, and adjectives. Students are expected to know this information. I think it is important information for students to understand and know how to use in their writing. I teach the parts of speech by having students sort the words we collect and post on the walls. I also ask my students to look in their own notebooks at the words they collect and see if they have a tendency to like one type of word more than another.

Activity

To begin the session, I tell the students, "We are going to sort the words on the wall by categories. We are going to use parts of speech to categorize these words. We will have nouns, verbs, adjectives, and adverbs. I want to know if you have a tendency to pay more attention to one type of word than another."

I begin sorting the words into these four categories. While I am sorting the words, I ask the students to think of descriptors that will help them remember each part of speech. Once I have sorted the words from the wall into these four categories, we discuss what they notice.

I ask the students to look in their writing notebooks for the types of words they collect. It is interesting to see what categories of words they like. They often comment that the type of book they are reading and the writing assignment they are working on determine which words they collect.

I put the words back on the wall collage-fashion.

I try to do this type of sort about once every four to six weeks. This opens up conversations to talk about parts of speech and how sentences are constructed.

Word Savvy: Integrated Vocabulary, Spelling, and Word Study, Grades 3–6 by Max Brand. Copyright © 2004. Stenhouse Publishers.

Posting Challenging Words

Materials

- Sentence strip or index card
- Dry-erase board
- Marker

Words That Typically Get Posted

another

beautiful

certain

different

especially

finally

important

necessary

possible

probably

really

separate

success

toward

usually

Thoughts

I teeter back and forth about the value of posting misspelled words on classroom walls. Over the years I have learned to become very selective about posting. Students will use the posted words if these words help with spelling struggles while writing or with decoding while reading. I keep track of words my students use frequently in their writing and often misspell, or the type of miscue pronunciations students have while reading. To get students to integrate the words into their thinking, I may demonstrate how I use the words during a shared writing or reading activity.

Activity

The steps to this activity are quite simple. I prepare a sentence strip and place it on the easel for all the students to see.

I tell the students, "As I have been looking through your writing, I notice that many of you have misspelled ——."

Next, I ask the students to say the word with me. We pronounce the word together, uttering it normally. Then I ask the students how many syllables are in the word.

Students guide my spelling of the word. We spell the word by syllables or word parts (onsets and rimes). While spelling a word, I often ask the students to first tell me the number of letters that word part has. I try to get them to visualize what the word looks like.

If a child miscues on the spelling of a word part, I use the dry-erase board to show the way the child said the word and to get other children to look at the word and identify if it looks right.

I then post the word in a place that all the students can see. I expect this word to be spelled correctly in everyday writing.

Word Savvy: Integrated Vocabulary, Spelling, and Word Study, Grades 3–6 by Max Brand. Copyright © 2004. Stenhouse Publishers.

A Day Full of Words

I write poetry like a reporter. I'm always looking for things outside of myself, taking notes about them. I have gone through life taking notes.

Sara Holbrook (Quoted in Graham 1999, 149)

ords have captured my attention for as long as I can remember. While I was a student, I daydreamed during vocabulary lessons because of the images the words brought to mind. While my own students are learning new content, it is my goal throughout the day that they learn to home in on and even become enraptured by words.

Let me take you through a day in my classroom once students have mastered our routines and rituals and we are comfortable together. This chapter chronicles a typical day toward the end of the first semester. We didn't study science on this day because we had just finished a unit. I try to balance the school day so that I teach all areas of the curriculum, but that can be an impossible task. The demands of special school programs outside of class pull my students many ways, but that doesn't stop me from developing a focused curriculum with the time we do have together.

There are multiple opportunities to integrate word study into the school day. Table 8.1 shows how I have tried to do this.

Table 8.1 Integrating Word Work into the School Day

Schedule	Word Work
Social time/DARE letters/Proofreading	Editing, revision
Content area read-aloud	Vocabulary and concept development
Social studies textbook reading	Decoding skills and strategies, vocabulary reinforcement, concept development
Math	Vocabulary and concept development
Poetry	Curiosity, ear for words
Read-aloud	Love of words, inferring word meanings, reading with an eye for word selection
Independent reading	Noticing and recording words, inferring word meanings
Word study	Spelling investigations, word features
Writing workshop	Using words as a tool for thinking and revising, using dictionary and thesaurus skills

Editing and Revision

The day begins at 8:55 a.m. Students filter in with five minutes of social time, emptying book bags so that homework can be turned in before chairs are taken down. The students settle into the morning by rereading their thank-you letters (drafted yesterday) to a police officer who recently visited.

The students notice editing and revision marks I have made as they locate and correct spelling and grammar errors. Common errors I noticed while reading the letters the previous evening are clarified in a quick focus lesson about 9:15 a.m., when all the students are accounted for. Then it is back to students' editing and completing final copies.

Finished drafts of letters begin showing up in the "finished" file tray about 9:35 a.m. The day formally starts at 9:45 a.m., as we all pledge allegiance to the flag. I share morning goals and the agenda. I ask if anyone has any thoughts or ideas before we dig in.

Laura speaks up to share a draft she has been working on at home. She has begun to work on an invitation for our poetry reading, which is three weeks away. Laura announces, "This is my first time writing an invitation for a poetry reading. While I read it, make sure it is clear. You know, how good we have gotten." Laura reads her draft (see Figure 8.1) as the

Figure 8.1 Draft of poetry flyer.

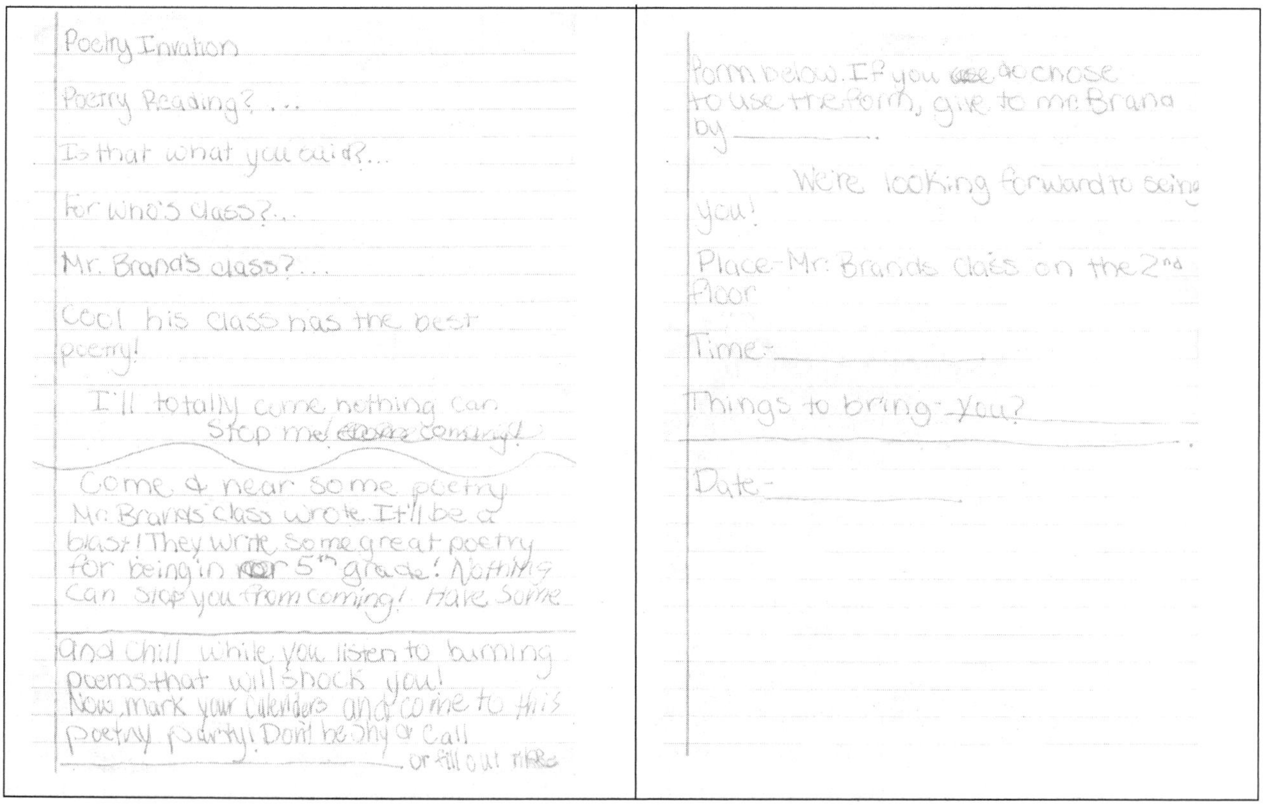
Poetry Invation
Poetry Reading? ...
Is that what you said?...
For who's class?...
Mr. Brand's class?...
Cool his class has the best poetry!
I'll totally come nothing can stop me! ~~from coming~~!
Come & hear some poetry Mr. Brand's class wrote. It'll be a blast! They write some great poetry for being in ~~our~~ 5th grade! Nothing can stop you from coming! Have some and chill while you listen to burning poems that will shock you!
Now mark your calenders and come to this poetry party! Don't be shy & call or fill out the
form below. If you ~~are~~ do chose to use the form, give to mr. Brand by ______.
We're looking forward to seeing you!
Place- Mr. Brands class on the 2nd floor
Time- ______
Things to bring- You?
Date- ______

Figure 8.2 Final verson of poetry flyer.

group listens attentively. Comments and suggestions swirl around the circle for the next few minutes.

Josh remarks, "I think it is clear, but you have too much on the page. It is hard to read on my own." Abby suggests, "Spread your thinking across the page like the poster for the movie *Holes*." Drake says, "Help the reader focus in on the big idea." The group applauds Laura, thanking her for taking on this task. The class decides that she should work up another draft during writing workshop so that they can revise it and send it home Friday with the class newsletter. Laura ends up shortening her draft, incorporating her classmates' suggestions. The final flyer is shown in Figure 8.2.

I then shift the students' attention to the day's social studies lesson. The social studies block begins with me reading aloud from *Plimoth Plantation* by Terry Dunnahoo. I read a short excerpt to provide some background knowledge about the difficulties of the journey to the New World. The children want me to reread the sentences, "The ship's timbers cracked and creaked. Water washed across the decks and leaked below, soaking passengers, their clothes, and their belongings" so that they can see if these lines are worthy of making it to our wall display of "lines that

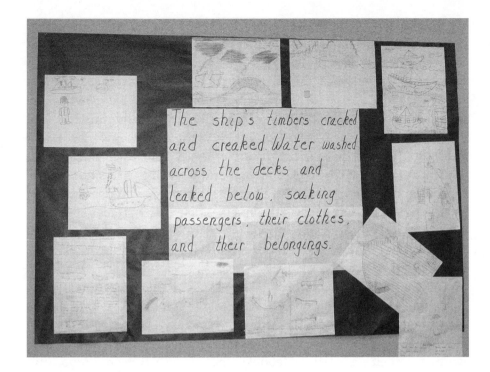

Figure 8.3 Sketches bring life to a description.

paint a clear image." We use the lines to do descriptive sketches (see Figure 8.3).

Content Words: Social Studies and Math

The children return to their seats and lug out their social studies textbooks. We prepare to read about Separatists, Puritans, Pilgrims, and the voyage of the *Mayflower*. We preview the social studies textbook by looking at pictures, maps, headings, and focus questions. We read words that require the pronunciation guide that is included in the textbook. Next, students ask questions about the text preview. Sydney asks how *Puritan, Separatist,* and *Pilgrim* go together as she previews the key vocabulary. Katie thinks that the book has misspelled the word *Separatist:* "Mr. Brand, it doesn't look right. In the second syllable it should have *er,* not *ar.*" A quick look at *separate* on a dry-erase board, and Katie is surprised that she has misspelled *separate* for some time. This leads to Chris's inferring that the Pilgrims were a separated group of people. He has a personal connection. The students read silently for twenty minutes and take notes. They are noting key words and phrases that help them understand the focus questions from each section.

During the silent reading time, I confer with students, supporting their reading and discussing the notes in their inquiry notebooks. I am interested in how they decide what is important. I am also interested in knowing where and why the social studies text is challenging. So I begin my conferences by asking, "How is the reading going?" I stop by Jackie's seat first because I know the text will stretch her. Jackie informs me, "The second paragraph here is tough, lots of vocabulary words together." I read it softly to her so as not to disturb others at her cluster. I notice that while I am reading, she copies *Puritan* and *purify* into her inquiry notebook. She adds *pure* to the list. "I get it. *Puritans* has to do with being pure," she says. "I see it now. It is much easier when you read it to me." Nick, within earshot, agrees with the idea of being able to see while I read it. I note that I may need to do more shared reading with the social studies text on the overhead.

When I know that all the children have read the assigned text once, we congregate with our notebooks in the meeting area. We form a cluster around the easel, focusing on the chart paper.

We close out the social studies reading by charting words that the students recorded in their notebooks that they felt were important. Confidently Jackie calls out, "*Purify*" as we begin to create the list of words:

> *purify*
> *Puritan*
> *Separatist*
> *separate*
> *Pilgrim*
> *holy journey*
> *Plymouth*
> *Virginia Company*
> *Virginia Colony*

I wonder how they have decided which words to write in their notebooks. "I wrote the Key Vocabulary words," Tyler informs the group. Melissa adds, "I read the focus question like you told us, and then thought about words that helped me understand the focus."

The discussion continues as students wonder about the idea of the focus question being an organization tool similar to what Melissa has suggested. I explain my thinking as to how I organize these words in my "notebook" (chart paper) so that I can answer the focus question of my reading. I show them how using the focus question—why and how the Pilgrims left England—helps me focus my thinking about what I read and notice words to help me understand this idea. Brad mutters, "Like a time line."

Then Kelsey steers the lesson off course a bit. She has noticed that *Separatist* looks and even sounds like *segregate*. She infers that the words have similar meanings. Both words have to do with separation. I write *separate*, *separation*, *segregate*, and *Separatist* on my small dry-erase board. I briefly reinforce the concept of root words and move on. I want to acknowledge Kelsey's connection to a word study lesson and the application, but not detract attention from the writing demonstration.

I have planned to demonstrate how to write a paragraph based on the reading and using notes. I am trying to help the students learn to summarize their understanding of their learning, a task they will be asked to do in a few months on a standardized test. I use words the students noted and recorded to write my paragraph. The paragraph focuses on why the Pilgrims came to the New World. I use shared writing to demonstrate thinking of how to go from a textbook to note taking, then to writing. This prepares students for the tests they will take in March as well as for a variety of writing and thinking tasks they will do throughout their academic careers.

Two things surprise me. First, the students want to copy my model and use this to study for the unit test. Second, Sydney and Morgan comment about what they learned. Morgan and others have a hard time reading and understanding textbooks. The girls comment that they feel more confident now that they have strategies to use while reading the textbook. They also reflect that they know why the *Mayflower* came to the New World.

The students filter back to their desks and dig out math materials. They focus on the screen, where I have projected a problem that requires the students to use their knowledge of vocabulary that we will use in our investigation into multiplication. "My age is a prime number. Last year my age included the factors 6 and 7. In two years my age will be a multiple of 5. How old am I?" While they read over the problem, I check in with Jackie and Nick, making sure they understand the problem. We discuss the important information in the problem and how it is signaled through words and phrases. I want to make sure that they do not confuse the idea of *multiple* and *factor*. These two terms have confused them and gotten in the way of their mathematical thinking. Then we talk about the mathematical reasoning they need to apply to this problem. At last the students begin working through the problem. Math continues for about an hour, and then math materials are stored away as they head off to Physical Education.

Finally, a moment to catch my breath and reflect on all that has happened this morning. I jot a few quick notes in my planning notebook. I make my daily visit to the office to drop off the PTO fund-raiser money and the handful of notes from parents explaining arrangements for

Student's Stretch the Sketch for Ralph Fletcher's "maple syrup buckets."

maple syrup buckets

At the edge of Mr. Wells's woods
I count eighteen rusty buckets
hanging from maple trees.

In these parts it's a known fact
that Mr. Wells has never smiled
in fact hardly speaks at all

Though he once explained to me
why it takes forty gallons of sap
to make a single gallon of syrup

Which made me wonder if maybe
He requires forty hours of silence
To make a single hour of talk.

He keeps bees, too: succulent honey.
Strange that such a sour man should
produce all that sweetness.

By Ralph Fletcher

after-school Girl Scout transportation that need to be stamped by the secretary. Back upstairs, I quickly check e-mail and homework while students are out of the room. I copy the earlier requested lines on sentence strips and add them to our wall of "lines that paint a clear image." Then down to the gym, and it's showtime again.

Ralph Fletcher's poem "maple syrup buckets" brings closure to the morning. The room is silent as I read the poem twice.

Chris breaks the quiet by saying Mr. Wells sounds like a character from the movie *Home Alone.* Josh challenges Chris, asking, "What words made you say that?" Chris's response catches me off guard. He says, "I think the poet wants me to think about how we view people. You know, get to know them." Laura adds, "Don't judge a book by its cover." "Yeah," retorts Chris. "That line about a sour man producing all that sweetness really got me to think that way. He really is nice but he is shy like me." The conversation is brief, and we will return to the ideas as I read the poem a few more times in the next few weeks. We share some quick thoughts about the morning, and then wash hands before lunch.

Reading, Writing, and Word Study

The afternoon has a pace far different from the morning's—deliberately slower. I am reading aloud Ann Martin's *Belle Teal.* Prior to the reading, Joseph brings up the word *haints* from yesterday's read-aloud. He is amazed at how Ann Martin has used a repeated phrase: "'Halloween,' scoffs Gran. She turns to the stove. 'Haints and ghouls . . . haints,' she mutters again, and shakes her head." *Haints* is making Joseph predict that there will be something that "haunts Belle" in this chapter. A conversation breaks out about what that horror could be. An Internet search during independent reading helped clarify our thinking as we discovered that *haints* is a southern term borrowed from Scotland. Mark Twain used *haints* in *Tom Sawyer.* Since a few of the students had seen the movie *Tom Sawyer,* they could infer that *haints* means "haunt."

While I read aloud, the children "think" in their reading notebooks. Most of the students have organized their notebook pages to keep track of language. We have decided that one category to note is word usage. Popular headings to help the children organize their thinking are "lines that paint a clear image," "lines that stick in my mind," "lines I wish I could write," and "words I want to remember."

Today the line that gets the children talking is "like peeking under a Band-Aid at a scrape." This is how Belle, the main character, describes looking at Big Boss. The words *peeking, Band-Aid,* and *scrape* elicit different perspectives as the children predict and infer what is happening at a critical point in the plot of the story.

After about fifty minutes, the reading and discussion of the chapter is complete. Prior to silent reading, I talk about how Michael and I have found a useful heading in his reading response log, "words I do not understand but I think are important." Michael explains his thinking to the class, and the children find their nooks and crannies as they snuggle

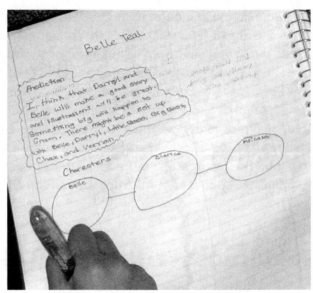

Two students organize their notes to follow *Belle Teal* in different ways.

up for the next thirty minutes with a book. I confer with a handful of students today. My conference focus is on goals that will improve understanding. I confer with five students, asking, "How are you using strategies discussed during read-aloud while reading today?" "How are you making sure you understand what you read?" "Will you use any of Michael's thinking?"

I sit down next to Matt, note that he is reading page 100 from *Frindle* by Andrew Clements, and then silently read over his shoulder. While reading, he pauses to write the word *endures* in his reading log. After he finishes writing this word, I ask him what he thinks the word means. Matt says, "I'm not sure I know how to say it. So I don't know what it means." I prompt him to try to pronounce the word. "In-dre," he tries. I coach him: "Try it again and think about the syllables." This time he pronounces *endure* correctly, emphasizing both syllables. "What do you think it means?" I ask. Laughing, he shrugs and says, "I don't know." We reread the letter from the text and I urge him to think about the phrase "all these years." "Ugh" is his response. I proceed to tell him I think it has something to do with lasting a long time: "A dictionary has lasted for a long time." "Like this word will last?" he asks. "Something like that, Matt," I respond. I quickly scribble a note that I may need to pull a small group during reading time for a focus lesson using context to help infer the meaning of unfamiliar words.

My next stop is Morgan. She has a few more strategies for trying to infer the meaning of unfamiliar words. She explains, "I read on. If it doesn't make sense a page or so later, I may go back. If not, lots of times

I just get it. I can't explain." I reassure Morgan: "Lots of times it is hard to put our finger on how we figure things out."

The children finish their reading and meander over to the easel area with pencils and word study notebooks in tow. Sydney, Laura, and Brad share words that caught their attention while reading and that they think should be posted as part of our class collection. I begin the day's word study focus lesson, telling the kids I noticed in their writing that words like *companion* and *opinion* were challenging their spelling knowledge. Then we generate other words from this knowledge. The students record these words in their word study notebooks. They leave the meeting area in search of their writing folders to finish writing poems for our poetry reading.

Midway through writing workshop, I stop the class to share Joseph's draft of his poem "Swan." I read yesterday's draft and today's revisions. I ask the students to note how by switching the order of some words, he created the image and thought he wanted (see Figure 8.4).

Jessica comments about how she was trying the same thing in her poem about not knowing how she upset her friend. Students go back to writing, and we have a quick session of buddy-sharing. Students put chairs up, and grab coats, backpacks, and mail from their boxes before heading out the door by 3:35 p.m. A normal day—too much to teach and never enough time to do it.

At 3:45 p.m., after a visit to my mailbox and a sip of water, the nagging question burns in my head, How much time can I spend at school today? I know I need to think about curriculum and planning, but this cannot overrun my life. The curriculum questions I toss back and forth in my mind will never be answered completely because each group of students is different. The more important question lingers about this time of day: Have I been a good husband, father, and friend?

Words. No matter what I think about when it comes to teaching, my thinking always takes me back to words. Teachers in our building, my friends in education, and teachers I meet during workshops—we are all constantly asking ourselves, Did I do enough?

Each time I get bothered by what I'm not accomplishing, I think of Melissa finally running up to me and smiling with her Cheshire cat grin, poem about female superiority in her hand, saying, "Guess what?" Baffled, I let her go on. "I used the dictionary without anyone telling me to." The same afternoon Joseph and Josh halt my reading of *Belle Teal* to argue that the character Darryl could not have shot Little Boss. At the height of their enthusiasm, I stop to ask, "Why did Ann Martin use the word *triumphantly* in the line, '"Because Darryl shot him,"' exclaims Vernon triumphantly'?" Joseph responds by commenting, "She's trying to throw our thinking off. She wants us to blame Darryl. That word was

Figure 8.4 Student's swan poem.

thrown in there to see if we are listening." Yes. They are listening, thinking, and paying more attention to words while they read and write daily.

Daily it feels like students come to me with some insight about word learning. They are questioning the author's use of a word or term. They hear a snippet of talk and find a place for it in their writing notebooks. They find a place for a word in a writing draft that they have been carrying around in their notebooks. They rethink their writing and change a word to express the image they are trying to get the reader to feel or think about. When this happens, I know my students are word-savvy.

A word-savvy student loves words. We cannot forget that intermediate-grade students are kids. Kids who like to play with words.

Appendix

Words Frequently Misspelled in Intermediate Grades

actually	*important*	*sure*
all right	*impossible*	*suspicious*
a lot	*independent*	*than*
also	*instead*	*that's*
although	*knew*	*their*
another	*know*	*themselves*
beautiful	*laugh*	*there*
believe	*necessary*	*they're*
brought	*occur*	*thought*
catch	*off*	*threw*
caught	*our*	*through*
certain	*piece*	*toward*
could	*possible*	*until*
definitely	*predict*	*usually*
different	*prediction*	*vary*
doesn't	*quality*	*wear*
enough	*really*	*we're*
especially	*recharge*	*whether*
everybody	*relate*	*which*
except	*said*	*would*
exciting	*should*	*wouldn't*
favorite	*something*	*write*
finally	*sometimes*	*you're*
heard	*special*	
hopeless	*success*	

Third-Grade Spelling (Self) Assessment

also

because

bedroom

between

couldn't

dripping

easiest

every

everybody

favorite

freedom

friendly

gallon

guessed

happiest

likely

passage

perhaps

planned

rainfall

should

skating

there's

trading

you're

Fourth-Grade Spelling (Self) Assessment

anything

cartoon

certain

closet

collection

council

development

discover

enforce

enjoy

everything

floppy

happened

happiness

important

journey

missile

notice

peaches

prediction

recycle

regularly

struggle

supplies

uneven

Spelling (Self) Assessment Grades 5 and 6

although	*used*
altogether	*with*
answer	*wouldn't*
brought	
build	
caught	
certain	
different	
during	
enough	
finally	
instead	
often	
perhaps	
possible	
pretty	
really	
scared	
shall	
should	
special	
stuff	
sure	
themselves	
though	
thought	

Spelling (Self) Assessment Grades 5 and 6

alligator

arrest

assign

autumn

balance

bomb

character

column

considerable

curious

desegregate

dessert

direction

doubt

especially

interrupted

often

opposite

patience

presence

probability

probably

sincerely

soften

until

Spelling (Self) Assessment Grades 5 and 6

abrasion

adaptation

delusion

description

designation

disinfect

disobey

documentation

enforce

enrich

forefather

forethought

happiest

hesitation

interruption

magician

misinform

naughtiest

preexisting

repossession

scariness

speechless

strangely

suppression

weariness

Bibliography

Children's Books

Aliki. 1996. *Those Summers.* New York: HarperCollins.

Allison, Amy. 2001. *Roger Williams, Founder of Rhode Island.* Broomall, PA: Chelsea House.

Borden, Louise. 2002. *America Is . . . .* New York: Margaret K. McElderry Books.

Brook, Donna. 1998. *The Journey of English.* New York: Clarion Books.

Bruchac, Joseph. 1997. *Many Nations: An Alphabet of Native America.* Mahwah, NJ: Bridgewater Books.

Burleigh, Robert. 1991. *Flight: The Journey of Charles Lindbergh.* New York: Philomel Books.

Carlstrom, Nancy White. 1997. *Raven and River.* Boston: Little, Brown.

Chin-Lee, Cynthia. 1997. *A Is for Asia.* New York: Orchard Books.

Clements, Andrew. 1996. *Frindle.* New York: Simon and Schuster.

"The Coral Reef Crisis." 2000. *Time for Kids* 6 (9).

Conrad, Pam. 1991. *Pedro's Journal: A Voyage with Christopher Columbus.* Honesdale, PA: Caroline House.

Dunnahoo, Terry. 1995. *Plimoth Plantation.* Orange, NJ: Bryant and Dillon.

Fletcher, Ralph. 1997a. *Ordinary Things: Poems from a Walk in Early Spring.* New York: Atheneum.

———. 1997b. *Twilight Comes Twice.* New York: Clarion Books.

———. 2003. *Hello, Harvest Moon.* New York: Clarion Books.

Ford, Juwanda G. 1997. *K Is for Kwanzaa.* New York: Cartwheel Books.

Furniss, Tim. 2000. *The Moon.* Spinning Through Space Series. London: Hodder and Stoughton.

George, Jean Craighead. 1995. *To Climb a Waterfall.* New York: Philomel Books.

Gerstein, Mordicai. 1999. *The Absolutely Awful Alphabet.* San Diego, CA: Harcourt Brace.

Gibbons, Gail. 1995. *Planet Earth—Inside Out.* New York: William Morrow.

———. 1997. *The Moon Book.* New York: Holiday House.

Graves, Donald. 1996. *Baseball, Snakes, and Summer Squash: Poems About Growing Up.* Honesdale, PA: Boyds Mills Press.

Gray, Libba Moore. 1995. *My Mama Had a Dancing Heart.* New York: Orchard Books.

Hesse, Karen. 1993. *Lester's Dog.* New York: Crown Publishing.

Hiaasen, Carl. 2002. *Hoot.* New York: Knopf.

Hooper, Meredith. 2001. *Who Built the Pyramid?* Cambridge, MA: Candlewick Press.

Horowitz, Ruth. 2000. *Crab Moon.* Cambridge, MA: Candlewick Press.

Janeczko, Paul. 2001. *A Poke in the I.* Cambridge, MA: Candlewick Press.

Leavitt, Melvin. 1995. *A Snow Story.* New York: Simon and Schuster.

Lerner, Carol. 1989. *Plant Families.* New York: William Morrow.

Locker, Thomas. 1997. *Water Dance.* San Diego, CA: Harcourt Brace.

———. 2000. *Cloud Dance.* San Diego, CA: Harcourt Brace.

London, Jonathan. 1999. *The Waterfall.* New York: Viking.

MacLachlan, Patricia. 1985. *Sarah, Plain and Tall.* New York: Harper and Row.

Maestro, Betsy, and Giulio Maestro. 1996. *The New Americans: Colonial Times, 1620–1689.* New York: Lothrop, Lee and Shepard.

Martin, Ann. 2001. *Belle Teal.* New York: Scholastic.

McDonald, Megan. 1999. *The Bone Keeper.* London: Dorling Kindersley.

McLoughland, Beverly. 1999. "Whippoorwill." In *Lives, Poems About Famous Americans.* Selected by Lee Bennett Hopkins. New York: HarperCollins.

McMillan, Bruce. 1992. *Going on a Whale Watch.* New York: Scholastic.

Merriam, Eve. 1990. "New Love." In *The Place My Words Are Looking For,* ed. P. Janeczko. New York: Simon and Schuster.

Miller, Debbie S. 2003. *Arctic Lights, Arctic Nights.* New York: Walker.

Mochizuki, Ken. 1993. *Baseball Saved Us.* New York: Lee and Low.

Montgomery, Sy. 1999. *The Snake Scientist.* Boston: Houghton Mifflin.

Morrison, Lillian. 1977. *The Sidewalk Racer and Other Poems of Sports and Motion.* New York: Lothrop, Lee and Shepard.

Murawski, Darlyne. 2000. *Bug Faces.* Washington: National Geographic Press.

Napier, Matt. 2002. *Z Is for Zamboni: A Hockey Alphabet.* Chelsea, MI: Sleeping Bear Press.

Nikola-Lisa, W. 2000. *The Year with Grandma Moses.* New York: Henry Holt.

Nyquist, Kate Boehm Jerome. 1994. *Exploring Space.* New York: Scholastic.

Osborne, Mary Pope. 1991. *Spider Kane and the Mystery Under the May-Apple.* New York: Knopf.

Paulsen, Gary. 1999. *Canoe Days.* New York: Doubleday.

Pinkney, Andrea Davis. 1998. *Duke Ellington.* New York: Hyperion.

Radunsky, Vladimir. 2001. *Table Manners: The Edifying Story of Two Friends Whose Discovery of Good Manners Promises Them a Glorious Future.* Cambridge, MA: Candlewick Press.

Ray, Mary Lyn. 1999. *Basket Moon.* Boston: Little, Brown.

Rylant, Cynthia. 1992. *An Angel for Solomon Singer.* New York: Orchard Books.

———. 1995. *The Van Gogh Café.* San Diego, CA: Harcourt Brace.

————. 2000. *In November.* San Diego, CA: Harcourt Brace.

Say, Allen. 2002. *Home of the Brave.* Boston: Houghton Mifflin.

Schonberg, Marcia. 2000. *B Is for Buckeye: An Ohio Alphabet.* Chelsea, MI: Sleeping Bear Press.

Schwartz, David. 1998. *G Is for Googol: A Math Alphabet Book.* Berkeley, CA: Tricycle Press.

Scillian, Devin. 2001. *A Is for America.* Chelsea, MI: Sleeping Bear Press.

Siebert, Diane. 2001. *Mississippi.* New York: HarperCollins.

Siy, Alexandra. 2001. *Footprints on the Moon.* Watertown, MA: Charlesbridge.

Snicket, Lemony. 2001. *The Hostile Hospital.* New York: HarperCollins.

Speare, Elizabeth George. 1958. *The Witch of Blackbird Pond.* Boston: Houghton Mifflin.

Swinburne, Stephen. 2002. *The Woods Scientist.* Boston: Houghton Mifflin.

Twain, Mark. 1876. *The Adventures of Tom Sawyer.* New York: Random House, 1999.

Van Allsburg, Chris. 1987. *The Z Was Zapped.* Boston: Houghton Mifflin.

Waber, Bernard. 2002. *Courage.* Boston: Houghton Mifflin.

Wick, Walter. 1997. *A Drop of Water.* New York: Scholastic.

Winer, Yvonne. 2002. *Birds Build Nests.* Watertown, MA: Charlesbridge.

Woodson, Jacqueline. 2001. *The Other Side.* New York: Putnam's.

Yolen, Jane. 1997. *Nocturne.* San Diego, CA: Harcourt Brace.

Yolen, Jane, and Heidi Elisabet Yolen Stemple. 1999. *The Mary Celeste.* New York: Simon and Schuster.

————. 2001. *The Wolf Girls.* New York: Simon and Schuster.

————. 2003. *Roanoke: The Lost Colony.* New York: Simon and Schuster.

Professional Literature and Reference

Allen, Janet. 1999. *Words, Words, Words: Teaching Vocabulary in Grades 4–12.* Portland, ME: Stenhouse.

Baker, Scott, Deborah Simmons, and Edward Kameenui. 2003. "Vocabulary Acquisition: Synthesis of the Research." <http://idea.uoregon.edu/~ncite/documents/techrep/tech13.html>.

Bean, Wendy, and Chrystine Bouffler. 1997. *Read, Write, Spell.* Portland, ME: Stenhouse.

Bear, Donald, Marcia Invernizzi, Shane Templeton, and Francine Johnston. 2003. *Words Their Way: Word Study for Phonics, Vocabulary, and Spelling Instruction.* 3d ed. Upper Saddle River, NJ: Prentice Hall.

Beck, Isabel, Margaret G. McKeown, and Linda Kucan. 2002. *Bringing Words to Life: Robust Vocabulary Instruction.* New York: Guilford Press.

Cambourne, Brian. 1984. "Language Learning and Literacy: Another Way of Looking at Language Learning." In *Towards a Reading-Writing Classroom,* ed. Andrea Butler and Jan Turbill. Portsmouth, NH: Heinemann.

———. 2002. "The Conditions of Learning." *The Reading Teacher* 55 (8): 758–762.

Ehri, L. 1992. "Review and Commentary: Stages of Spelling Development." In S. Templeton and D. Bear, eds., *Development of Orthographic Knowledge and the Foundations of Literacy: A Memorial Festschrift for Edmund H. Henderson,* pp. 307–332. Hillsdale, NJ: Lawrence Erlbaum.

Fletcher, Ralph. 1993. *What a Writer Needs.* Portsmouth, NH: Heinemann.

———. 1996. *Breathing In, Breathing Out: Keeping a Writer's Notebook.* Portsmouth, NH: Heinemann.

Fountas, Irene, and Gay Su Pinnell. 2001. *Guiding Readers and Writers Grades 3–6: Teaching Comprehension, Genre, and Content Literacy.* Portsmouth, NH: Heinemann.

Ganske, Kathy. 2000. *Word Journeys.* New York: Guilford Press.

Graham, Paula. 1999. *Speaking of Journals.* Honesdale, PA: Boyds Mills Press.

Graves, Donald. 1994. *A Fresh Look at Writing.* Portsmouth, NH: Heinemann.

———. 1999. *Bring Life into Learning.* Portsmouth, NH: Heinemann.

Henderson, Edmund. 1990. *Teaching Spelling.* Boston: Houghton Mifflin.

Lamott, Anne. 1994. *Bird by Bird: Some Instructions on Writing and Life.* New York: Anchor Books.

Leu, Donald Jr., and Charles K. Kinzer. 2002. *Effective Literacy Instruction K–8.* 5th ed. Upper Saddle River, NJ: Prentice Hall.

Murray, Donald. 1985. *A Writer Teaches Writing.* 2d ed. Boston: Houghton Mifflin.

———. 1996. *Crafting a Life in Essay, Story, Poem.* Portsmouth, NH: Heinemann/Boynton-Cook.

Nagy, William. 1988. *Teaching Vocabulary to Improve Reading Comprehension.* Newark, DE: International Reading Association.

Patton, Michael. 2002. *Qualitative Research and Evaluation Methods.* 3d ed. Thousand Oaks, CA: Sage.

Pearson, P. David, and M. C. Gallagher. 1983. "The Instruction of Reading Comprehension." *Contemporary Educational Psychology* 8: 317–344.

Phenix, Jo. 2004. *The Spelling Teacher's Book of Lists.* 2d ed. Portland, ME: Stenhouse.

Ray, Katie Wood, and Lester Laminack. 2001. *Writing Workshop: Working Through the Hard Parts (and They're All Hard Parts)*. Urbana, IL: National Council of Teachers of English.

Smith, Frank. 1988. *Understanding Reading.* 4th ed. Hillsdale, NJ: Erlbaum.

Stevenson, Harold, and James Stigler. 1992. *Learning Gap: Why Our Schools Are Failing and What We Can Learn from Japanese and Chinese Education.* New York: Summit Books.

Tekiela, Stan. 2002. *Birds of Ohio: Field Guide.* Cambridge, MN: Adventure Publications.

Tharp, Roland, and Ronald Gallimore. 1988. *Rousing Minds to Life: Teaching, Learning and Schooling in Social Context.* Cambridge: Cambridge University Press.

Vygotsky, Lev. 1934. *Thought and Language.* Rev. ed., ed. Alex Kozulin. Cambridge, MA: MIT Press, 1986.